TALE OF
THE LOST DAUGHTER

Karen Clark

SheBard Media Inc.

Clark, Karen 1961-

ISBN 978-0-9936919-0-4

Grateful acknowledgement is made for the following:
She Changes Everything chant, by Starhawk. Used by permission.
The Inanna/Ereshkigal myth in Chapter 3, *Darkest Night*, is based on The Electronic Text Corpus of Sumerian Literature translation of *Inanna's Descent to the Nether World*. Black, J.A., Cunningham, G., Fluckiger-Hawker, E, Robson, E., and Zólyomi, G., The Electronic Text Corpus of Sumerian Literature (http://www-etcsl.orient.ox.ac.uk/), Oxford 1998- .

This book is a work of fiction. Names and characters are products of the author's imagination. Any resemblance to actual persons, living or dead, are entirely coincidental. Salt Spring Island is a real place but the events described are fictional.

Cover design by Shelby Johnstone.
http://www.shelbyjohnstone.com

*For Hecate and those called to Her mysteries,
and for my beloveds, Larry and Nathan.*

CHAPTER 1

SOUL ACHE

The winter twilight sky edged into my corner office on the twenty-eighth floor of a glass and steel tower in the heart of Toronto's financial district. She appeared as if out of thin air, a jet black raven staring at me through the plate-glass window, with small, dark, intelligent eyes that sparkled with tiny, star-like flecks of light.

I blinked several times to make sure this wasn't a hallucination induced by the excesses of my earlier corporate luncheon. No such luck, she was the real thing, bigger and more regal than a common crow, with a sleek beauty and slight luminescent sheen to her inky feathers. Her harsh, lonely cries seemed to come from some other place, echoing and insistent, three and then two calls repeating slowly, as if she waited for a reply.

Normally I wouldn't have spared those eyes a second glance. I don't do nature. I do shopping. I do restaurants. I do all-inclusive resorts. I do personal trainer and power yoga. Mostly I do work, sixty to seventy hours a week. But not birds or beasts or green growing things. Yet on that evening, at that particular moment, a chasm opened in me that I could not deny, and this feathered ally arrived to point my way home.

How else can I even begin to explain what propelled me on this strange adventure? Three short days ago, December 17 to be exact, I was leading a perfectly normal life, and now, in the waning daylight hours of December 20, I'm bouncing about in a flimsy, six-seat floatplane, with spindly metal supports and cigar-shaped pontoons for landing gear. My destination is a barely populated, forest-covered rock on the Canadian West Coast, a place I didn't even know existed last week.

A wild, glorious panorama surrounds me — craggy, charcoaled mountains, mist-shrouded islands and the undulating expanse of a dark green sea. The passenger beside me, a balding man in a bedraggled, navy blue overcoat, stares out the window with a dewy-eyed expression of Zen-like bliss. But I can't sit still; I cross and uncross my legs, bumping up against icy steel on one side and my neighbor on the other.

Maybe this place is more beautiful than the grumpy, gray wintertime of Toronto, but the winds holding up this insubstantial plane seem to have taken on a predatory howl, and that frigid, bottomless ocean doesn't look too welcoming either. Of course the cute pilot with the charming French accent, just one seat in front of me, is a nice bit of distraction, but good looks don't guarantee talent behind the wheel.

"We are hitting a small patch of turbulence," the pilot says, "Nothing to worry about. There's a bit of blustery weather moving through, and it's always squally when we pass over Galiano Island."

An involuntary gasp slips through my pursed lips as the plane suddenly jostles from side to side, like a tinkertoy in the rough hands of a giant. Acrid sweat pools in my armpits. I grip the armrests and will myself to stay calm. No one else is freaking out, only me. I breathe slowly and deeply, in and out through my nose, just like in yoga class. Do people die in these things? No, no, otherwise there would have been some kind of legal disclaimer on the website or at least a few life insurance ads. An old John Denver song pops into my head, one my Opa Kass used to play for me when I was a kid. For a few moments, John's crooning about a Rocky Mountain high soothes me, and then I remember that he crashed into the ocean in a plane as small as this one.

A steady, shaking change in altitude marks the beginning of our descent, and the floatplane, miraculously, is still in one piece. I peer through the window, my burgundy-painted nails carving half circles into my tender palms. White-tipped waves reach hungrily toward us, threatening and then delivering a bone-rattling, graceless landing. We smack through the chop, bumping our way to a stop alongside a weathered dock shared by a collection of rain-drenched watercraft, ranging from luxury yachts to sturdy fishing boats, but bereft of human occupation.

Welcome to the middle of nowhere. No work, no friends, no night life and no Starbucks coffee. Really, why did I come to this off-the-grid place? No, damn it, no! I won't go down that road. I'm here and I need to trust myself. Some primal instinct has drawn me to this island, like a parched camel to an oasis. But at least a camel knows it thirsts for water. Me, I haven't the faintest idea what I'm after. Only that I ache for something missing from my life, somehow linked to my soul — a noun only recently, and uncomfortably, activated in my vocabulary. Yet, undeniably, I sense that whatever nourishment I crave exists in this unlikely place so far from the world that I know. Whether or not this is sheer madness or trusting myself, here I am, following the directives of the peculiar, inky raven that visited me last Friday at the turning of day into nightfall.

Lunch had indeed been a foray into excessive indulgence on that fateful Friday, at least for most of my fellow revelers. Frosted rays of sunshine poured in from large bay windows that framed a snow-dusted, downtown Toronto skyline, further brightening the lacquered, crimson surfaces of the restaurant's Asian décor. The event was our senior management Christmas festivity and an early celebration of our best financial performance in TechStar's ten-year history — not the happiest time for our company but definitely the most lucrative.

Last year, TechStar bought out a rival investment firm, Lead Digital, with a plan of capitalizing on the companies' differing strategies for investing in promising internet technologies. TechStar provided venture capital in the early stages of a new company, whereas Lead Digital purchased shares of emerging top players in the global marketplace. On the surface, the merger appeared to offer complimentary approaches, but on the ground it was like forcing two wolf packs to live in the same territory, with the requisite snarling and displays of supremacy en route to establishing a new alpha order.

Like most corporate environments, everything simmered beneath the surface and played out in backroom politics — a pretty façade with plastic smiles that disguised cutthroat dynamics and deadly fangs. This lunch was a prime example: a fat-cat feast of fusion dim sum, where overflowing trays of Christmas-themed cocktails and vast quantities of miniature bamboo baskets spoke of our shared good fortune and God-granted right to spend and gorge as we pleased. I soon lost track of the exotic dishes, puffing out garlic- and ginger-scented steam clouds, that made their journey from linen-draped trolleys to the indiscriminate palates of my blue-suited cohorts: Peking duck ravioli, crab and taro spring rolls, lemongrass-infused scallop dumplings, hoisin barbeque ribs and numerous other elaborate concoctions that didn't reach my end of the table.

Matt, Techstar's CEO, founder and principle shareholder, reigned over us at the head of the table. As usual, Matt stood out as the jewel in the crowd, not only because of his turquoise shirt and tie, and exquisitely tailored, charcoal suit, but because he rose above the corporate politics, beaming his sparkling, green eyes and boyish grin on each of us in turn. But then again, as the big boss with a brilliant financial track record, Matt no longer had to fight for territory with the rest of us.

At the other end of the table, not-so-subtly positioning himself as second-in-command, Trent, the partner from Lead Digital, surveyed our group with steel gray, rapacious eyes. A corpulent, ruddy-skinned man with a voracious appetite for anything that crossed his path, Trent wolfed his way through a loaded plate of these delicacies in the time it took me to finish a small serving of dumplings. Every time his glance happened in my direction, his pink tongue slowly passed over his thin lips. Despite my overwhelming urge to slap that smug, predatory look off his face, I did not lose my smile or look away.

The rest of our party lined up along the sides of the table, roughly clustered in TechStar and Lead Digital groupings. In total there were eight men and me, the lone, but definitely not token, woman. Not that there weren't other women in our outfit, but only I had made it into the rarified, testosterone-laced air of upper management. My closest female competition, Marsha, our Human Resource Director, was inherited from the Lead Digital ranks. But she wasn't high enough in the pecking order to be invited to the Christmas luncheon.

Marsha seemed to hate me from our very first encounter at a meet-and-greet between our two firms prior to the merger. I noticed her checking me out with a scathing stare from across the room. She shifted to an insipid smile and offered me a limp, perfunctory handshake when Matt introduced us. Shortly afterwards, we were thrown together in the near-impossible task of reorganizing our joined, incompatible companies.

As the last of the dim sum dishes were cleared away, and yet another round of cranberry red and neon green drinks were delivered to our table, Matt rose to address us. After the compulsory congratulations on our fiscal performance, Matt sprung his surprise announcement. Steve, my boss and Matt's long-time partner and financial guru, was retiring and moving to Costa Rica.

At first there was stunned silence and then a round of loud, boisterous applause. I took the measure of the crowd and sensed the odd mix of blind admiration and greedy jealousy. Steve had made more money in his twenties than most of these guys would make in their lifetime. He was leaving behind miserable winters, rush-hour traffic, ten-hour days and weekends at the office, and watching his hairline recede with every passing year. Now Steve could write his own ticket, whiling away his days in luxury and dabbling in Costa Rica's budding tech sector.

But Matt and I knew the whole story. The double whammy of his second divorce shortly after his forty-third birthday and the unrelenting stress of sharing the firm's leadership with Trent had seriously compromised Steve's health. High blood pressure, insomnia, depression and a steady diet of antacids — Steve's doctor had warned him to make some serious changes or he'd be sleeping on the underside of the grass before he was fifty. This wasn't self-chosen, retirement bliss. Steve was the first casualty of our merger: a high-level, painful loss for TechStar and a clear victory for Trent.

Steve stood up, steadied himself against the table and took

a sip of water before speaking. I was probably the only one who noticed the dark circles under his eyes, the extra gray in his hair and his pasty, clammy complexion. No, not true. Trent never missed a thing; his self-congratulatory smirk told me that he knew exactly why Steve was stepping down. He had hunted his prey for twelve months and now he had felled him, annihilating Matt's favorite and his closest competition.

"Matt has given me the honor of announcing my replacement," Steve said, "It shouldn't surprise any of you that Sarah Ashby will be assuming my partner role as TechStar's Chief Financial Officer." Then turning in my direction, he continued, "Sarah, it's been one of my greatest pleasures to work with you these past six years. You have given your all to this company. There is no one better suited to take my place and help lead TechStar into its next phase. Not only do you know our side of the business inside and out, through your central role in the reorganization you also understand where our merged company is heading. To your success, Sarah, I know you will continue to be a star!"

My throat tightened and I blinked back a few tears. The pride in Steve's voice and the steady way he looked at me were genuine; he meant every word he said. He had recruited me, a fellow Harvard MBA and native New Yorker, enticing me to seek my fortune on Canadian soil with the promise that neither gender nor age would stand in the way of my quick rise to success. I'd kept my part of the bargain, leaving behind my beloved New York and giving most of my waking hours to TechStar. And so had Steve, championing and mentoring me from the get-go for the top management team.

Steve shifted to face the rest of the group and then said, "Let's drink to our new partner, Sarah. Don't let her youth and beauty deceive you. She has more brains, drive and killer instinct than the rest of us put together. And more good grace and class as well. To Sarah!"

I raised my glass demurely in response to my companions' obligatory applause and canned laughter, but I took only a small, measured sip of my drink while everyone else downed their glasses.

Thirty-three, female and a partner in a multi-million dollar company, I sat still and straight as a statue, once again assessing the reaction of the group. I glanced at Trent; there was no surprise on his face. He already knew why I occupied the seat of honor between Matt and Steve; Matt had confirmed Steve's retirement and my promotion with him earlier this morning. Trent locked his eyes on mine and by the nasty curl at the corners of his mouth I understood that he'd be after me next. There was no way he was going to knock me off my corporate throne this early in the game. I tipped my head, smiled sweetly and then stood to address the group, willing my body to relax and my voice to come out steady and strong.

"Thank you, Matt and Steve, for this fabulous opportunity," I said, "We'll miss you, Steve. I won't pretend that I can fill your shoes, but I'll work my hardest to ensure our continued success. And though I wish you all the happiness you deserve in your new life, don't think you can slip from our grasp so easily. I see our next Christmas lunch amidst swaying palms with you briefing us on Costa Rica's investment opportunities."

More obligatory applause and laughter followed my remarks as I took my seat. Only Matt's and Steve's enthusiasm seemed genuine as they beamed their unconditional approval at me. There was something else in Matt's look, a momentary blaze of heat that made my heart race and my cheeks flush, and then, just as quick, it was gone.

The other male faces froze in tight-lipped smiles, while they looked me up and down, taking in the not-too-revealing cut of my white linen shirt, the half-empty, lipstick-rimmed cocktail glass at my place setting, and Steve's hand resting paternally on my shoulder. I didn't serve them coffee at office functions. I ran boardroom meetings where they weren't invited. I smelled good, walked nice, looked pretty, but talked smart and produced moneyed results, and never uncrossed my legs for anyone in the office. My mother, a successful business woman in her own right, taught me early on that sexual allure in the workplace was like expensive perfume: a dab will do and never let a co-worker dip into your bottle.

But office gossip didn't deal in reality, only speculation. Although I knew that a few people suspected that I was sleeping with Matt or Steve, or both, no one ever dared to say this out loud until Marsha arrived on the scene. I knew Marsha had been spreading rumors by making off-handed, insinuating comments to the support staff that spread through the ranks like wildfire. Not that anyone said anything to me directly, but I sensed that my co-workers looked at me differently; nothing I could pinpoint, other than a touch of disrespect from the women and a subtle, sexual come-on from the men. Through a few well-placed innuendos, Marsha had tarnished my reputation and hard-won accomplishments in the eyes of these men, with no apparent damage to her own character.

I continued through the rest of the lunch, drinking, joking and accepting firm-handshake congratulations from this pack of alpha wolves, with my facial muscles locked in a mask-like smile. All the while, my senses registered the over-spiced, over-hyped food, unnaturally vivid drinks, and the palpable envy that hung in the air like suspended drops of acid, wanting nothing more than to slip into my cocktail and burn me dead from the inside out. Although Marsha was physically absent, my thoughts couldn't help but turn to her. Matt hadn't advised her of my rise to partner status and she was going to freak out when she heard the news secondhand. What new heights of backstabbing and troublemaking would my promotion drive her to?

Trent approached me as we all rose to leave. Under the gentleman-like guise of helping me on with my coat, he leaned in, his breath stinking of garlic and gin, and whispered in my ear, "Let's see how you stand up in the big-boy's league, little Sarah, with no more Steve to baby you."

And then, taking a leisurely look down my shirtfront, he said, "But I'm sure working with you has its perks — at least that's what I've heard."

The bastard! The god-damned bastard! Acid boiled in my guts as I scrambled for a scathing response. But he had planned his attack perfectly and slipped amongst the departing Lead Digital crowd before I could utter a word. And in the next moment, Matt had sidled up beside me.

"I want you to take some time off before the new year," Matt said as we stepped from the overheated restaurant into a cold blast of winter wind.

"You're kidding?" I said, stopping mid-sidewalk to confront him, "You've just promoted me and you want me to take a leisurely Christmas break? What about the reorganization project with Marsha? What about getting my replacement sorted out before January?"

"All of that can wait. I want you fresh and well rested before you move into Steve's office," Matt said, "He's clearing up any remaining issues on his plate and I know you don't have anything pressing on yours. Besides, if you hang around I'll insist you trade places with Elsa and wear that velvet elf outfit to hand out presents at the office party."

"Yeah right, as if you could?" I said as we started walking again, weaving our way through the afternoon crowd.

"Think about it, okay?" Matt pushed, "You could use a break and it would make me feel better to know you had a nice, pleasant holiday before pulling up a chair with Trent and me."

Matt didn't say anything else; maybe he couldn't give voice to his real concerns about my new working relationship with Trent. I was a big girl after all and I'd accepted this promotion with no illusions about corporate dynamics. I didn't say anything either, not a word about my Marsha misgivings nor Trent's aggressive moves on me. But I did agree to think about his vacation offer and to let him know before Monday. I didn't have substantive plans for the holidays, other than my traditional Christmas brunch with Opa Kass at his senior home and my best friend Jules's New Year's party. My mother's idea of Christmas was sending me a postcard from somewhere hot. This year she was off to Belize to bake in the sun with her latest boyfriend. Maybe a bit of downtime wouldn't be so bad.

Back in my office, with a slow-building MSG headache for company, I spent a few hours tidying up my work and dealing with outstanding issues, just in case I took Matt up on his holiday offer. When I was done, I leaned back in my chair and smoothed my hands over the bare expanse of my desk, drinking in that curious sense of wellbeing that an ordered space always seemed to engender. Outside my door the place was silent, except for the hum of the florescent lighting; everyone else had fled the corporate nest for the weekend.

From my top drawer, I pulled out the single sheet of paper with my job offer and hefty remuneration package — salary, bonus and stock options — printed in bold font. I read and then re-read the letter, three or four times, and then stared at the page expectantly, patiently, waiting. For what, I didn't know — a flutter of excitement, a sigh of satisfaction, maybe even an uncharacteristic victory bellow, anything to mark this long-anticipated moment of success? But it did not come.

Drip, one tear slid down my cheek, splashing on the page in my trembling hands and smudging the ink imprint of my seven-figure income into black streaks. Drip, drip, one followed another and another, wet, raw, inexplicable. And then a floodgate opened within me, pouring out of my constricted throat and pounding through my flesh in a torrent of noisy, heaving anguish. Waves of sobs rose and fell in sharp jags of keening — sounds my body couldn't possibly make — had never made before. I held back nothing, howling myself empty and limp, like someone had pulled out all my bones and left a jellied puddle on my desk. Absolute, impenetrable silence followed, as if the whole world waited with bated breath for what would come next.

From a still, calm place somewhere within the secret folds of my heart, a gentle voice arose saying, "Sarah, slow down, open to the in and out movement of your body with breath. Look inside, below the below of what you know, into the depth of who you are. What you seek waits for you there."

My spine straightened of its own accord, sitting me up tall, alert, enervated. I rubbed away my tears and carelessly wiped my sniffling nose on the dark sleeve of my best Prada suit. My consciousness expanded, as if a light had been turned on, and I peered, for the first time, into the vastness of my inner landscape. A nameless, formless hunger rose up and sucked me into its vortex, squeezing all the air from my lungs and thoughts from my mind, leaving me gasping like a beached fish, yet also wonderfully open and empty.

A gift of pure, crystal-clear awareness bubbled up into this emptiness that spoke to me in simple, strange words, but with a power I couldn't deny, "You can no longer hide from me. I am your soul ache, come to guide you home."

Tap, tap, tap. Tap, tap, tap. I turned to the tinted panel of glass that covered one wall of my office. A web of ice crystals had spread across its surface, painted by the chilled exhalation of a December wind. An enormous, jet black raven perched on the narrow, metal ledge outside my window, haloed by the neon glow of a waking urban nightscape. Her hot breath melted a portal through the icy web into my world. She looked crafty, purposeful, as she called insistently and shifted from one leathery foot to the other, dancing her darkling shadow across the polished sheen of my desk. In my expanded state of awareness, the raven's arrival seemed commonplace, expected.

I slowed my breath and opened to the fathomless depth of the raven's twinkling, obsidian eyes. As if by magic, her rasping cries melted a portal into the icy interior of my heart, frosted over by the chilled exhalation of my unrelenting drive, and other deeper, hidden hurts that I could sense but not name. And in this melting, a secret desire awoke within me, a yearning for something essential missing from my life, connected to my soul. An understanding passed between us, a promise that I would follow whatever path this raven and my soul laid before me.

With a nod of her feathered brow, the raven extended her wings and leapt from the ledge, catching an updraft and vanishing, in the blink of a moment, into the spreading cobalt blue of the evening sky.

Early the next morning, I dreamt that I bent to pick up a black feather. As I touched its stiff, hollow quill, I heard the distant, raucous cry of a raven, enticing me forward and deeper into the dreamscape. I clutched three more feathers in my other fist — magic trail markers that guided me, Hansel and Gretel like, toward some destined place. And that was it; I woke up and the dreamscape, with its salient details of the fated location, crumbled into dust. I had a fleeting vision of me desperately chasing after the dissipating mists of the dream, my hungry hands trying to catch hold of the ephemeral vapors. But it was no use; the dream was gone. All that remained was the tickling, teasing sensation of my fingertips touching that final feather.

Damn, what did this mystery bird want of me? First a flesh and blood raven dropped by for a twilight visit outside my office window, communing with me somehow and extracting a promise that I would follow where she led. And now this dream raven showed up to entice me on a journey, but didn't have the common decency to reveal the destination.

On impulse, I jumped out of bed and dressed myself from head to foot in midnight black, in honor of my newfound raven acquaintance. In reckless abandonment of standard practice, I managed to compress my beautification routine into a miraculous ten minutes, applying a bare minimum of makeup and skipping my hair styling entirely. Then I stepped out of the cherry red door of my red-brick Victorian townhouse, my breath billowing in rapid, little vents of steam, into the crystalline brilliance of a sun-crisped winter morning.

I traipsed through the tree-lined streets of my tony neighborhood — the historic, downtown enclave called the Annex — with the vague notion of following the trail of those black feathers in the dream. Christmas lights still twinkled in multicolored hues from rooflines and window frames, waiting for waking homeowners to turn them off for the day. Tiny, brown birds flittered between gray, winter-bare branches, shaking loose miniature dustings of snow as they fluffed up their feathers against the press of winter. I walked at a leisurely pace, the ice-crusted sidewalks crunching beneath my boot heels, all the while scanning the sky and the ground for signs of my raven dream. When I reached Bloor Street, a distance of three good-sized city blocks from my home, nothing had shown up to direct my travels — no raven, no black feather and no flash of intuition.

So where to next? Nothing came to me. I stopped in my tracks, my face crunched up in concentration. A blast of wind nipped at my exposed skin and pierced the finely woven fabric of my pants. Didn't I have something more constructive to do with my time? Maybe some presents to wrap? Laundry to iron? Nails to paint? Anything other than this ridiculous nonsense? What was I doing wandering about aimlessly in the dead of winter, dressed for fashion not the elements? And where indeed was I headed with all of this?

My belly grumbled loudly and I laughed out loud. Here was the answer of where to go next. I turned west on Bloor Street toward the tantalizing fresh-baked goods and dark-roasted coffee of my favorite breakfast stop only two blocks away.

Those two blocks felt like an eternity, with each step strained, like pushing through an invisible barrier stretched tight between opposing forces. One force held me back, determined to resist these strange, new notions. The other urged me forward toward the secret desires awakening in me, for what I really didn't know, other than I was on the trail of something to do with my soul. But even these impulses grated on me. I mean really, since when did I indulge in this kind of new age mumbo jumbo? Spiritual matters had never really made it onto my list of worldly concerns and held about as much sway in my life as the politics of Karl Marx.

As my brain began to throb, threatening a full-blown tension headache, I reached a compromise. I gave this dream adventure until the end of breakfast to come up with some bit of evidence that I hadn't lost my mind — no feather, then no more listening to ravens.

Jazz strains of Christmas standards and a blanket of pastry-scented, warm air enveloped me as I opened the door. A big chalkboard listed the daily coffee and breakfast specials, and woven baskets filled with sweet and savory baked treats lined the polished wood shelves. The place was already bustling, with three staff rushing about to serve a long line of patrons at the front counter. I looked around, despairing of finding a seat, when a pair of friendly eyes and a broad smile snagged my attention from a sunlit table close to the windows.

"I was wondering how long it would take you to notice me," Jules said, "I've been here for a half-hour, hoping you'd walk through that door. Saturday morning and cinnamon buns — when it comes to food you're pretty predictable!"

Though it had taken me a few minutes to notice Jules, she had clearly already captured the attention of two twenty-something young men. They sat backwards on their window-front stools, smiling invitingly in her direction, apparently oblivious, or uncaring, that she was a good decade their senior. But Jules only had eyes for me. I slipped between the tables to join her and she wrapped me in a big hug, as soothing and welcoming as the sweet aromas radiating from the bakery ovens.

Jules worked as an executive assistant for Lead Digital's management team and joined our company as part of the merger. Not long after, she showed up at my yoga class and I couldn't take my eyes off of her. Neither could anyone else in the room, men and women alike. Her skintight, fire red outfit had something to do with it, clearly distinguishing her from the black-yoga-wear conformity of the rest of us. The outfit accentuated her flawless, creamy white skin, thick, auburn mane of hair and toned, long-limbed form. But even more captivating was the intensity and beauty of her poses. This woman completely inhabited her body and moved with a sensual, cat-like grace, all liquid muscles and quivering power. Yet Jules never seemed to notice others' attention. This morning was no different.

With barely a pause for breath, she said, "I wanted to cross paths with you this morning so I could treat you to a victory breakfast. Congratulations! Wow, Matt made you a partner! Marsha was in a complete snit. She was fuming about being the Human Resource Director and not even being consulted. Ha! Serves her right for being so nasty to you!"

Among the many things we bonded over, like our shared love of food and art, our mutual disdain for Marsha was high on the list. Jules was as compelling and colorful with words as she was with her appearance. Her favorite, most vivid description of Marsha was a zombie from the realm of the walking dead, with a pasty complexion, tight-lipped slash of blood red lipstick, and a smell of wood rot with musty, floral overtones. Actually I saw Marsha as more toad-like, with her short, squat body, strangely flattened features and eyes that bulged ominously when she was driving home her point. Because of the Marsha factor, we kept our friendship private from the office.

"Marsha started up again with the Matt and Sarah love-affair storyline," Jules said, scrapping her chair legs across the polished concrete floor so as to fully face me, "She was going on about how this promotion proves that you've been fooling around with him. A gorgeous bachelor, no current girlfriend, your obvious mooning whenever he is in the room — easy enough to put the pieces together in Marsha's warped mind. I mean, you couldn't have been made partner because you're brilliant, Steve's right-hand person and a key player at Tech-Star."

"I don't moon over Matt," I said with a slight frown.

"Come on, Sarah," Jules countered with a good-natured poke to my arm, "You do have a wee crush on the man. And so does every other woman in the office, even zombie-face Marsha."

A vision of the blazing flash in Matt's green eyes at yesterday's lunch came back to me. My heart once again quickened its beat and a delicious, tingling sensation spread through my thighs. Had I been secretly lusting over Matt? Is that why I never kept a boyfriend for longer than three months? And why I hadn't even mustered up a date for Jules's New Year's party? The guys I dated were never smart enough, good looking enough, charismatic enough or ambitious enough. Perhaps not Matt-like enough? Come to think about it, Matt never seemed to keep a girlfriend for more than three months either. What if Marsha was partially right? Maybe there was a mutual attraction between Matt and me, though we had never acted upon it. Rather than dwell on these uncomfortable thoughts, I changed the subject.

"Oh, Jules," I said, rubbing the creases in my brow, "I'm really sorry I didn't let you know sooner, but Steve's retirement was top secret. And I've had a lot on my mind since the announcement, so I forgot to call or text you."

Jules squeezed my hands in hers and for a silent moment stared into my eyes.

"Is something wrong?" she asked gently, "You don't look well. If you don't mind me saying, your grooming isn't up to standard. Since when do you leave the house without combing your hair?"

I didn't laugh or make a grab for my mirror, and Jules quickly turned serious again.

"I've never seen you like this," she said, reaching to brush back a stray lock of hair, "I hope this isn't about me. I was thrilled to hear your news, regardless of who told me. Or about Marsha, she can't touch you now you're a partner. Anything she says will sound like sour grapes."

My stomach grumbled and churned uncomfortably. For most of my life, I'd hoarded my secrets and kept the sharing of personal, private information to a minimum. But Jules was by far the best friend I'd ever had, with the exception of my Opa Kass. If I could trust anyone with my current angst, it was her. I looked around the room, fidgeting with my hands in my lap. The place was still busy, but everyone close to us seemed caught up in their own world. Jules's two admirers had left. The young lovers at the next table were feeding each other tidbits of apple tart. A gray-haired man across from us, in a camel-colored sweater that had seen better days, had his face buried in the Saturday paper.

I took a deep breath and then said, "This isn't about either of those things. It's a bit of an odd story. Could we order breakfast and then I will fill you in?"

Between mouthfuls of fresh berries, yogurt and warm cinnamon buns, I blurted out the whole story: my unexpected, emotional meltdown, the encounter with the raven outside my office window, and the subsequent raven dream with its seductive images of way-showing feathers and an undisclosed destination. Jules didn't interrupt me once, though I saw questions flash in her eyes and rise to her lips.

"I'm losing it, Jules," I said, welling up with tears, "I've sacrificed most of my adult years to my career, following in my dad's footsteps and working like a dog. And now that I've made it and landed a job that would even make that critical bastard proud, I'm blubbering on about my soul and listening to self-help advice from a raven. These can't be the actions of a sane person."

Jules got up to refill our coffee and perhaps to gather her thoughts before responding to me. When she returned, her earlier exuberance had stilled to a quiet, steady calm.

"Your dad may have been the president of an engineering firm, with a big salary, big house and all the right social connections," she said, wiping away a glistening tear from my cheek, "but he barely paid attention to you when you were growing up and then he dropped dead of a heart attack when you were only sixteen. Maybe a part of you knows better than to follow blindly in his footsteps."

"But where can this possibly lead?" I said, my voice coming out in a squeaky croak, "What if I do find these feathers? What then? God, Jules, I've just taken on a huge job. Now is not the time to be setting off on a spiritual adventure that is sure to mess with my head. You know as well as I do that Marsha is not the only one hoping I'll make a mistake. Trent has already made it perfectly clear that he is after my blood. You should've seen how he looked at me at the senior management lunch. He wants my head on a platter. One slipup or sign of vulnerability and I'm dead meat."

"I know you live for your career," Jules said, "But there are things that matter more than goose-stepping to the rules made by the likes of Trent and Marsha. Life can't be ordered by category and color, like your closets and cupboards. I love you dearly, but I worry that you're a wee bit too uptight and in control for your own good. Sometimes things have to get messy. Sometimes you have to get a little wild, a little crazy, to really be alive."

Out of my peripheral vision, I saw the woman seated beside us get up to leave. She had silver hair, the color of moonlight, and ageless, sienna-toned skin. It was odd that I hadn't noticed her in my earlier scan of the room. We turned to each other for a brief moment; the sparkle in her amethyst eyes and the hint of mischief in the upturn of her lips instantly entranced me. My heart opened and my inner turmoil stopped.

Without a word, she dropped a brochure on our table and then headed out into the frosty winter air. It was from one of my favorite Toronto hangouts, the Art Gallery of Ontario, or the AGO in local lingo. The front page featured a traveling exhibit from the Vancouver Art Gallery. Even with my limited knowledge of Canada's geo-cultural map, I knew Vancouver was a West Coast, urban destination for the spiritually minded and most certainly a raven hangout. I felt a faint, downward fluttering sensation in my gut and then a soft, tingling touch, as if something as light as a feather had come to rest inside me.

"The first feather," I said to Jules, pushing the AGO brochure in front of her.

Jules turned to the door but the woman had vanished. Then she gingerly ran her fingertips over the brochure.

"How do you know?" she asked with a wide-eyed look that mirrored my own disconcertion at this sudden turn of events.

"I don't know," I said, "Something in the woman's look when she left the brochure on our table told me it was a clue. And then I had an odd sensation in my belly when I saw the visiting exhibit from Vancouver."

"Things just got a little wilder," Jules said with a quick grin, "Are you going to go?"

"Yes. I have to. Can you come with me?" I asked as I pulled on my coat and grabbed my purse.

"I can't. I'm so sorry," Jules said as she also stood up to leave, "I promised my Aunt Lily a month ago that we would have a Christmas shopping day together. It would break her heart for me to cancel. Besides, I think you need to figure this one out on your own."

Thirty minutes later I stood, my whole body rigid and alert, before a riveting, modernist canvas entitled "Big Raven" in which the artist, Emily Carr, depicted a larger-than-life raven gracefully awaiting its death and return to Mother Earth. In that moment an alternative reality, one where ravens talk, direct your dreams and show up in breathtaking paintings, truly kicked in. This stuff was not a fantasy game I'd cooked up for my entertainment; it was real, scary real.

I stared at this oil-painted masterpiece of the West Coast mythos, absorbing the vibrant, bold strokes of the down-flowing radiance of sky and the swirling, momentary embrace of flesh and forest, with the raven, earth-anchored and heaven-reaching, suspended between the two. My own flesh hummed with these big, untamed, primal forces that danced my heart to an erratic, cacophonic beat. My hands clenched and unclenched at my sides. Terror and delight, equally present, equally powerful, coursed through me, leaving me paralyzed in doubt and confusion. One part of me fumed and sputtered that this was utter nonsense, spiritual pap for the weak minded, and that I should squeeze my eyes shut until it all went away. The other, breathing heavy, legs spread wide and fingers reaching out hungrily, knew good food when she saw it — soul food that she had been waiting for her whole life.

Emily Carr was a passionate, free-spirited woman who refused to be domesticated by the Victorian strictures of her early years, or to let her spirit and magnificent originality be broken by the backwater isolation of her Canadian West Coast home and the misogynist ethos of her times. All around me her masterworks spoke of her feral, ardent communion with the forest and the earth-rooted aboriginal culture in a language that I have always innately understood: the capturing of energy, color and beauty in art form.

"Fuck your tidy ways," I heard her whisper through the palpable, wild otherness reaching out from her canvases, "Fuck your fears. Be bold. Be brave. Be free."

Feather number two, this one plucked from the oil-painted back of Big Raven, fluttered down into my belly and rested beside its ebony sister.

Feather number one had pointed me in the direction of the West Coast. Feather number two suggested a location closer to Victoria, Emily Carr's hometown located on Vancouver Island, a large island off the British Columbia mainland. A slow, delicious smile spread across my face, melting the tension in my jaw, as my thoughts turned to feather number three and the possibility that it held the secret destination of my raven dream.

After a few hours of hanging out with Emily Carr, I visited yet another of my favorite foodie spots: a small vegetarian restaurant not far from the AGO that served the best split pea soup I've ever tasted, along with thick slices of dark rye. As always, I ordered the soup and nestled into my preferred seat, a russet leather chair and walnut table tucked beside a street-level window. The tasty food set before me calmed my buzzing speculation about the next feather.

When I finished my lunch, I dug out the New York Times Sunday edition from the bottom of the pile of international newspapers that this restaurant stocked to entice customers to linger over a cappuccino and one of their plate-sized gingersnap cookies. No matter that it was Saturday and this was last week's paper, I enjoyed connecting with my New York hometown.

I reached the travel section on my final bite of ginger cookie, brushing off the sugar crystals clinging to my thumb and forefinger, and then smoothed out the paper to peruse enticing foreign locales. The week's travel column, "36 Hours," featured Salt Spring Island: "A forest and ocean-bound paradise not far from Victoria, British Columbia, with a Saturday market, kayaking, hiking and a thriving, local cultural scene."

For the third time that day, a woman acted as intermediary for the dream raven and her black feather directives.

"Oh my God," my server burst out, pointing a black-polished fingernail at the article I'd just finished, "I'd give a year's worth of tips to visit that place. My boyfriend cycled there last summer and said he'd never seen bigger, smarter birds than the local ravens — not like our city crows always pecking away in the trash — these are real, wild beasts, fearless enough to steal a sausage right off your plate."

As she reached to clear away my dishes, her bicep crossed my field of vision, along with its muscled tattoo of a blue-black raven, and, without thinking, I ran my fingertips slowly, tenderly, across this inked, feathered form. Rather than take offense at my boldness, the young woman smiled at me and pulled up her short sleeve to give me an unobstructed view of her raven body art.

"Magic," I said, more to myself than to her.

"Trickster," she added, "Sure to lead you down paths you wouldn't choose for yourself; ravens can see things that you can't and know things that you don't."

A cawing, mischievous burst of laughter echoed in my inner ear as my server moved on to the next table.

This third feather didn't even have time to twirl down and

join the other two in my sated belly before I pulled out my iPad and started making travel arrangements: a Monday morning flight from Toronto to Vancouver; a late afternoon floatplane from Vancouver to Ganges Harbor on Salt Spring Island; a deluxe holiday package at a waterfront specialty hotel called the Hastings House; and my return travel arrangements four days later to get me home in time for my Christmas date with Opa Kass. All the while my neural impulses moved faster than my mind and I deliberately blocked my internal tsunami of naysaying shrieks of, "What the hell are you doing? Have you totally gone mad? You can't do this!" I hit the last key, confirming the credit card data for my hotel reservation and sealing my fate, and then released my pent-up breath in a long, loud exhale. Jules was right — sometimes things have to get a little wild, a little crazy.

A few e-mails tidied up the remaining details: one to Matt accepting his offer of an extended Christmas break, telling him I'd be out of town until December 24 and asking him to let me know if anything important came up in my absence; another to my Opa Kass's senior home asking them to let him know I'd be away and providing them with contact information in case of an emergency; and a final one to Jules with the cryptic text, "The raven feathers have spoken. I'm off to the Wild West — Salt Spring Island — the Hastings House. Hope I return with my sanity intact. Thanks for being you."

Perhaps I should have called and spoken to each of them in person, especially Opa Kass, but I didn't dare. Maybe it was superstition; you're not supposed to speak your wishes out loud, and my dearest wish was to make this trip. In my gut I knew this to be a once-in-a-lifetime invitation that I could not, would not, shut down. Because if I did, I was certain that something precious and irreplaceable would be lost forever.

For better or for worse, I was headed west to Salt Spring Island.

My fourth and final feather was waiting for me on my stone-slab doorstep when I arrived home — nine inches long, with a rounded tip and an olive green sheen where it caught the fading afternoon light along its glossy, ebony surface. I picked it up and pressed it to my lips as warm, silver tears descended down my cheeks and splashed onto the hard, frozen earth.

The pilot hops onto the dock and secures the floatplane as the other passengers gather up their belongings. For the umpteenth time, I stroke the silky, flat surface of the black feather that I've kept within touching distance since I found it on my doorstep on Saturday afternoon. It's the only hard, physical proof that I didn't imagine all the wacky events that have landed me on Salt Spring, a place as far off the beaten track as I've ever been before. I brush the feather once more for good luck and then tuck it into my leather notepad holder.

The plane, dock, pilot and passengers sway and rock between the forces of wind and wave. I grip the pilot's out-stretched hand as he guides me down the narrow metal steps. When my feet make contact with the slippery, wooden planks, he ushers me to one side with a nod and a friendly, dare I say flirty, wink. I smile in return but not with the poised certainty I usually display with the opposite sex. Somehow I can't pull it off, between my wobbly legs and overpowering urge to drop to my knees and kiss the green-tinged dock in gratitude for our safe arrival. I murmur apologies as he lugs my two stuffed-to-the-brim suitcases from the minute storage space behind the seats. I've most definitely surpassed the twenty-five pound baggage limit — a fine-print detail I overlooked on the floatplane website in an uncharacteristic display of sloppiness. My bags got to accompany me after I paid a hefty fee for my excess.

I pause for a few moments, taking in the surrounding sea, landscape and Ganges town center which abuts against the docks. Within the stretch of those brief moments, I find myself alone as the other passengers confidently stride off and the pilot revs up the engine and quickly disappears into the blustery skies. The silence presses in on me, well not exactly silence because the blowing wind and lapping whitecaps make their own kind of music, but I detect barely a trace of the ever-present bustle of people and traffic that usually comes with human occupation, nor the stink. I suck air through my nose in boisterous, noisy sniffs and my lungs greedily expand as if they can't get enough of this briny, earthy, oxygen-rich concoction. No yellow smog, no industrial squalor and no dog crap-stained snow; actually no snow at all or biting drafts or stripped-bare branches. A bald eagle, with wide-spread wings, circles overhead and then lands in the olive green finery of a fir tree. Where do they hide the Disney crew who remake this place for the arrival of tourists?

The Disney fantasy evaporates as the squalling winds condense into fat, cold raindrops that run down the inside of my coat collar and plaster my hair to my head. A dense dampness creeps along my skin and roots itself in my bones. I totter along the slippery docks in four-inch heels and skinny jeans, destabilized by the laptop and purse strung around my neck, and my ungainly baggage. Cracks between the wooden boards open like small, gaping mouths ready to bite into my spiked footwear and send me toppling into the frigid sea that froths and splashes only two feet away on either side. I reach the end of the dock, short of breath but without calamity, and confront my next insurmountable challenge. The street perches a good fifteen feet above my head, reachable only by a steep metal ramp. With these boots and that incline, it's just not going to happen.

I scan the street, hoping for assistance, but there is no one in sight. The weather must have driven everyone inside. A pitter, patter, pitter, patter of shuffling feet on a metal roof draws my gaze upward. A single raven, with a rain-slicked, feather coat, peers down at me from a fire-engine red rooftop — my welcome party braving these miserable weather conditions. Head tilted to the right, she stares at me with glistening, pebble eyes, seeming to size up my situation before taking wing.

Within a heartbeat, I hear a baritone voice from the top of the ramp say, "Are you looking for a cab?"

"Oh yes, yes please," I reply, hoping he won't notice my pitiable vulnerability and stiff me on the fare.

To my relief, the raven has delivered me into the hands of a gentle giant who effortlessly herds me to shelter in the worn backseat of a silver, 1990's-era Toyota cab, surprisingly free of the ravages of time and rust. Rain and a slow-rising fog obscure the view outside the car windows. The rattling heater warms my dripping, chilled exterior. Five minutes and six dollars later, we pull into the graveled drive of the Hastings House, with me mesmerized en route by the undulating, indigo star constellation tattooed on the muscled neck of my rescuer. I slip him a ten-dollar bill and tell him to keep the change.

My cab driver escorts me to a rustic, cedar building that houses the reception area. Bleary-eyed and desperate for a blow dryer, I tumble through the doorway and collapse onto a brown leather chair, with my luggage sprawled around me. A mascara-stained rivulet dribbles down my cheek and my shoulders give in to a slovenly bow.

A little girl, with a dark blonde ponytail and a sunshine yellow raincoat, turns and smiles at me; there's a wide gap where her two bottom front teeth should be. A shabby, damp teddy bear, missing one eye and small patches of brown fur, dangles from her left hand. With her other hand, she rubs the sodden nap of my tan suede coat, now morphed into a soggy shade of chestnut brown.

"You don't look so good," she says with an adorable lisp, "My mom says we have to dry my bear as soon as we get to our room or he is going to catch a cold. You better do that too."

"You're right," I say, "If I get a cold, I won't have much fun. I'm Sarah. What's your name?"

"I'm Emilie," she says, "My bear's name is Fredrick. He doesn't like Freddie, so don't call him that. That's my mom and dad. We live in Alberta, but my granny and grandpa live in Victoria. We're going to visit them for Christmas after we spend a few days in this fancy place. What are you up to?"

"You know, I'm really not sure," I say, "I guess I've come here for an adventure and then I'm going back to Toronto to be with my grandpa for Christmas Day."

"Oh Salt Spring is good for adventures," Emilie says, "My dad says there are fairies and treasure and all kinds of magic stuff here. But no ghosts or scary things."

Emilie's parents join us, both of them tall and slim with the same hue of dark blonde hair as their daughter, though the father's is liberally peppered with gray.

"I hope our Emilie isn't talking your ear off," the father says after introducing himself as Ted and his wife as Beth.

"Not at all," I say, "I needed a new friend today."

With my luggage in tow, the porter guides me along a gravel path to the Post Cottage, a quaint, two-room suite in its own ocean-view building, separate from the main guest accommodations in the Manor House. The rain has stopped and a dense fog parts as we move through, offering small glimpses of the emerald green, immaculate landscape on either side of the path.

Not more than thirty minutes later, I'm rosy-skinned from a steamy shower and snuggled into the luxuriant, snow white folds of a hotel robe. The gas fireplace fills the small sitting room with radiant warmth. The muted, lavender shades of early evening spill from the double French doors onto the West Coast feast spread out before me on fine linen and bone china. I reverently tuck into a bowl of saffron-tinted bouillabaisse. According to the waiter who delivered my room service, the chef makes the stew with halibut, scallops, shrimp, mussels and Dungeness crab caught from the ocean waters not far from my door; and with garlic, tomatoes, leeks, fennel and a touch of orange zest, or so my nose and tongue joyfully report after my first few spoonfuls. Between mouthfuls of stew and crunchy bites of French bread, I savor a fine Bordeaux, enjoying its rich, burgundy hue as I swirl it in my wine glass and letting its relaxing warmth settle my nerves.

I barely finish the last drop of broth and sip of wine before my eyelids begin to droop. Soon I slip under the starched sheets and a downy duvet. In a shadowy corner of my mind, a part of me wants to shake me awake for a few moments longer and remind me that one good meal doesn't make up for the weirdness of this place, nor the fact that I'm an urban fish out of water, floundering about like an idiot in this wet, green-tinted wonderland. But I don't rise for the bait; a meal as good as tonight's can make up for just about anything. And on that pleasant thought, I slip dreamily into the undertow of sleep.

Chapter 2

Lost and Refound

In the hazy, pink shades of early dawn, a sultry, warm voice wakes me, "Sarah, my sweet Sarah, open your eyes and your heart — awake. Your journey begins today. Your soul ache has led you here and now you must follow your instincts and find your way home to your true self."

I don't know where this voice comes from, whether from inside or outside of me, but the words fill me with tender thoughts of my beloved Opa Kass.

Opa hadn't been much of a father to my father. In my growing-up years, they rarely spoke more than a few words, and my father complained that his dad was a hard-driving bastard who cared more about his laundry business empire than his only son. Well the fruit didn't fall far from the tree. Both my parents were obsessed with their careers and left my base, physical needs to a revolving door of caregivers. It was Opa Kass who watched over my fragile heart and budding selfhood. He sold his laundry business not long after I was born, and perhaps he showered me with the adoration and attention he denied my father.

As a child I spent every Sunday with Opa, exploring museums, art galleries and New York's best restaurants, or hanging out at his Long Island house making food and art. Opa was in his late seventies when I moved to Toronto. With my Oma and my father dead, he only had me to love and care for him in his declining years, so I brought him with me and settled him into an exclusive senior residence not far from my townhouse. I rekindled our Sunday visit tradition and we spend long afternoons visiting and talking about nothing in particular: the latest book he is reading, our favorite New York memories and sometimes my work.

Wrapped in a fleece blanket, soft as kitten fur, I step outside the French doors of my hotel suite and into a serene landscape of green grass, soft-lapping waves and a lightening sky. I turn east, in the direction of the delicate, orange rays of the rising sun, and imagine my waking awareness reaching out across the distance to my Opa. Even with me all grown up and him fading, our tending roles reversed, still my whole being seeks out sustenance and comfort in our connection.

"Opa Kass," I whisper, "I know you're far away, but you're the only one I really trust to understand me. And to love me enough to know that what I'm doing is good and right, even if it doesn't make any sense. I'm traveling way, way outside my comfort zone, Opa. And it scares and excites me. I know that I have to do this and that's all that matters. I have to do this."

I sense his withered hand in mine, squeezing my soft, warm flesh and letting me know he is by my side.

A seemingly random childhood memory plays across my mind, of Opa Kass and me in his backyard on a sunlit, summer afternoon, playing the sniff-detective game.

In this game I was blindfolded, he placed something from his garden under my nose, and I had to guess its identity based on scent alone. After sifting my way through surface wafts of pungent earth and the lavender soap on Opa's skin, I recognized the tangy snap of an unripe apple.

"That's cheating, Opa," I said, laughing, "The apples aren't even in season yet."

In the long hours Opa Kass and I spent wandering in his flower and vegetable gardens, I developed this unusual skill. I could detect the subtle differences in scent between raspberries, blueberries and strawberries, tell a carrot from a parsnip, and identify every species of flower that flourished under his beneficent care. Three correct guesses earned me a chocolate bar — proof of the essential role of the right motivator on any path to mastery. I depended on this skill in my growing years, smelling my way into good friendships and away from bum dates.

Later, in my job, I earned the moniker of "The Nose" in honor of my less-than-scientific, but amazingly accurate ability to sniff out successful investment prospects. Matt and Steve discovered this odd gift of mine purely by chance. We were about to give a new project the green light — the social media platform looked fantastic, the core staff members had all the right credentials and other financial backers were lined up. The company's founders met in our boardroom with Matt, Steve and me to talk through the final details. I'd never encountered these men face-to-face, and when the younger of the two shook my hand, my nose started to twitch uncomfortably. For the rest of the meeting, I struggled to concentrate; my adrenalin system fired, "danger, danger," and my whole body trembled with the urge to take action.

As soon as they left, I stated point blank, "This is a no go." Matt and Steve thought I'd lost my mind because the day before I had been the project's biggest champion. But I simply said, "One of them stinks. Trust me." Three months later, the company went bust when the junior founder ran off with the start-up funds.

From that moment on, Matt and Steve called upon "The Nose" to cull the sweet investments from the stinkers, usually through a lunch date with the key players. By an unspoken agreement, we never told anyone else in the company about my secret skill. Perhaps we all understood the damage this personal bit of weirdness could do to my reputation for financial acumen, especially in the hands of Trent and Marsha.

The boisterous scolding of a feisty, gray squirrel, skittering up and down the trunk of a gnarled, leafless tree, brings me back to the present moment on Salt Spring. I instinctively take in several deep, silent breaths and settle into the unique scent configuration that is the living out-breath of this place. I draw the air through my flared nostrils, like a connoisseur sipping a prized vintage, and savor its nuanced aromas. The moist, cool breeze carries an invigorating tang of sea and coniferous trees, smoky tendrils of wood fires and the faintest hint of fresh-brewed coffee. Although I can't name every element of such a complex mix of human habitation and wild things, I trust my body's primal response to the mysterious pheromonal dance that only my nose understands. "Yes," my nose says, speaking not in words nor a twinge of muscles nor a firing of a part of my brain, but more as a wave of awareness that flows through me and lets me know that this place is good and right for me.

My muscles soften, releasing the lingering tension in between my shoulder blades and in my lower back from yesterday's trials. I'm not a fool stumbling in the dark after all. I may be urban blind in this natural environment, ignorant on the gross measures of right footwear and packing requirements, but I have other skills and allies to guide me in this foreign land: my new raven friend, my love connection to Opa Kass and my own innate sensing of good from bad.

I bow to the fragrant breezes and changeling winds, sending

my thanks out into the world, and then shut my door on the cold dawn to ready myself for the adventure ahead.

A series of gravel and stone-paved pathways, bordered by a close-cut lawn, link the various buildings that make up the Hastings House resort. The Manor House, an English-style country home that wouldn't have looked out of place in a Jane Austen novel, holds court in the center of the property. A short jaunt along the path takes me from my Post Cottage suite to the dining room in the Manor House.

I settle at a table for two, haloed in soft winter rays that sparkle off the glassware and encircle me in their warm glow. Wide mullion windows frame a picturesque view of a curved, rocky coastline fringed with giant, overhanging evergreen trees, and a flat, calm expanse of black-green ocean dotted with sailboats at anchor. In the distance, I see a cluster of low buildings that must be the Ganges downtown core, and behind this, green slopes against a backdrop of a blue-gray, cloudless sky.

A cup of steaming coffee, rich-hued against the bone white china, soon appears in front of me. An omelet follows, made with eggs so fresh I swear I can hear the mother chicken clucking her distress at her missing offspring. A locally made goat cheese oozes between the fluffy folds and melts on my tongue. I dive into my meal with an unladylike ferocity.

On my second cup of coffee, I lean back and savor the view. Sunlight illuminates diamond-like raindrops captured in dense clusters of fir needles. Small, black-capped birds flit from branch to branch, their tiny beaks opening and closing in the secret songs of their feathered kin.

"I love those birds," my little friend Emilie says, startling me with her sudden appearance at my side, "They look like they're wearing superhero masks. My grandpa says they're chickadees."

"My grandpa used to teach me about nature when I was little," I say, turning to face Emilie.

"Do you know a lot about birds and plants and stuff?" Emilie asks.

"I used to," I say with a slight frown, "but I forgot about those things when I grew up."

For a brief moment, I sense the insatiable curiosity of my long-ago girl-self who spent countless hours poking her nose into every vibrant, multi-scented corner of the outdoor world. Then she is gone and my heart squeezes down tight on the empty space left behind.

Emilie has already moved on to another topic, "Come say hi to my mom and dad. You don't want to be all lonely by yourself."

Without waiting for an answer, she zigzags between the tables, beaming her contagious grin at everyone she passes, and leads me to her parents' table at the other end of the restaurant.

Ted and Beth don't seem surprised to find a stranger in their family circle.

"Emilie has taken a shining to you," Ted says, "When she spotted you across the room, she wanted to say hello."

Their place settings have been cleared of dishes, but Emilie's breakfast — a plate of waffles, strawberries and whipped cream — appears to have been abandoned mid-meal.

"Sarah looks really pretty," Emilie says as she starts back into her breakfast, "and much better than yesterday."

"That's our Emilie," Beth says, laughing, "Never afraid to speak her mind. You have had quite the transformation. That outfit fits so well, it looks like it was sewn right onto your body."

"Well thanks!" I reply with a smile, "Today felt special, so I tried extra hard to look nice."

"Like the first day of school," Emilie says.

"Yes, exactly the same," I say.

"Today's a special day for me as well," Emilie says, licking strawberry-tinted whipped cream from her fingertips, "We're going on a real treasure hunt, aren't we daddy?"

"Absolutely," Ted says, "They say there's fairy treasure up on Mount Erskine. But we'll have to be very, very quiet or the fairies will vanish and we'll never find their homes."

"And we have to leave them a gift," Emilie says, "You can't take fairy treasure without giving something good back."

"What are your plans for the day?" Beth asks.

"I don't know. I haven't really got any," I reply, "I think I'd like to check out Ganges and get my bearings."

"Why don't we give you a lift into town?" Beth says, "We could meet you at the parking lot in an hour, if that works for you."

I explore the beach on the way back to my cottage. A broad swath of barnacle-encrusted rocks marks the receding tide line. Miniature crabs, in camouflage colors of pebble gray and seaweed green, scuttle in every direction as I overturn a flat rock with the tip of my boot. I bend down and peer into a tidal-pool village of intriguing creatures: mottled green sea anemones with fibrillating, pink-tipped protrusions, teeny, speckled fish darting away from my shadow, and black snails leisurely sliming their way over the sandy bottom.

The peaceful swish of waves on the shore is interrupted by loud honking. I look up to see several Canada geese rushing toward me, with extended wings and hissing, pink tongues — elegant birds with a mean, and apparently territorial, attitude.

I stumble backwards and then turn and flee to the safe haven of my room, sidestepping the green-brown piles of their droppings, with them nipping at my heels.

An ache begins to pulse behind my eyes and I rest my forehead against the cool interior glass of the French doors. The geese have lost interest in bullying me and have gone back to foraging for their breakfast, but they have blasted open a Pandora's Box in me. Trent and Marsha — I have tried to push them out of my thoughts since I booked my trip to Salt Spring. Matt e-mailed me back on Sunday, thrilled that I had accepted his holiday offer and clear that I should forget about TechStar for the next two weeks, but it's not so easy.

Gallivanting off on a little West Coast adventure doesn't change office politics. Trent is on the hunt for me, no doubt about it. Marsha will be only too happy to aid him; she's always sucking up to him and she's toxic in her own right, with an established propensity for poisoning my work relationships and personal accomplishments at no cost to herself. Even Matt appears to have bought into her corporate-cheerleader façade, and he is usually a shrewd judge of character. My rich breakfast starts to roil uncomfortably in my stomach. What damage are those two getting up to in my absence? And what was I thinking, leaving the field just as the battle for territory is about to begin?

I crumple onto the couch in the sitting room and curl my body around my aching belly. Damn, I can't do this right now. I can't straddle two worlds. Maybe I'm safe from their mischief for awhile. Nothing happens in the office at the end of December, and surely I can bask in the protective glow of my promotion, at least while it's still shiny and new in people's minds. Matt and Jules will let me know if there's anything to worry about.

"Fuck your fears," isn't that what Emilie Carr's paintings said to me, "Be bold. Be brave. Be free." Jules said much the same thing when she called on Sunday, "Don't screw this up, Sarah. Leave your tidy life behind and ride your edge for these few days. Big things happen to those who dare."

I pull my cell phone from my purse, grab my laptop from the desk and stash them in my empty suitcase — no work and no Toronto-life distractions, at least not today. Something else rumbles in my belly region, an aching, gnawing hunger that has nothing to do with food. It rises up through the center of my body to the top of my head and pushes everything out of my mind except one thought — a treasure hunt, for something precious, for lost jewels — yes, yes, thank you Emilie, that's it! I don't need to know what I'm looking for, or even why; I only need to follow where my soul ache and this wild hunger lead me.

A treasure hunt — giddiness tickles my heart and lights up my face with a little-girl grin — that's my plan for the day. I'll follow my nose and my whims and see what happens. Ganges is a small country village and I'm pretty sure I can't go too far astray.

With the town's grocery store at my back, I turn full circle and take in a smattering of stores and restaurants. The buildings are of a pleasing, human-sized scale, no more than two stories high. Natural views peak through in every direction: steep, evergreen clad hills encircle the town on one side and the ocean on the other.

I detect none of the usual urban markers: no parking meters, no traffic lights, no congested intersections, no homeless people and no McDonald's golden arches. A mom leisurely pushes her stroller across the crosswalk, waving at the waiting drivers: a young guy in an old, dusty, maroon pickup truck and a well-groomed, middle-aged woman in a shiny black SUV. Actually everyone seems to smile and wave at each other, and look you straight in the eye as they pass by, including me, a complete stranger gawking at the world.

A white building with a small clock tower catches my fancy and I walk toward it. This turns out to be the fire station with freshly washed, red trucks gleaming in the late-morning sun. A firefighter tips his hat to me as I make my way to a grassy area sandwiched between a broad promenade and the ocean. From my internet research, I guess that this must be Centennial Park, home to the famed Salt Spring market. In the summertime, this place is filled with colorful stalls of organic produce, baked goods and the eclectic creations of local artisans. But the market is closed until the spring and the park has a wintry, sleepy feel, with its empty space interrupted only by a couple with matching dreadlocks smoking something that I suspect is not a cigarette, and a guy throwing a chewed ball to his golden retriever.

I sit down on a park bench to rest and take my bearings, hunching up my shoulders as a damp, sea-laden breeze works its way under my wool scarf. Across the street, the gentle strumming of a street musician, singing an old Neil Young tune, sets me on a new course. But before I can find the source of the music, my nose kicks into gear and redirects me. At first I'm drawn to the beckoning smells seeping under the doorframe of a chocolate and gelato store. I press up against the window and take in the pastel colors of chocolate mint, organic lavender and lemon sorbet, and the shelves lined with intricately shaped chocolate and candied treasures.

"Enticing yes," my nose tells me, "but no, not here, keep going."

A few more deep sniffs and I'm tracking again.

"Cinnamon buns," my radar announces, "Past the cars, across the creek and up the stairs."

Without question, I follow these directions, egged on by the promise of my favorite treat, and find myself at the threshold of Barb's, a funky bakery and restaurant. With a loud plunk, a brawny raven lands on a wooden table in the outdoor seating area and struts toward a seed-encrusted chunk of bread. My little-girl grin widens and my whole body tingles as I reach for the door.

I order a matcha latte and a cinnamon twist and then perch myself on a stool at a small, round table. From here I garner a clear view of the glass door, the bakery and coffee counter, and the oak tables and chairs of this busy eatery. One bite of my twist and a quick look around tell me that I've simultaneously discovered a veritable masterpiece of cinnamon-dusted pastry and landed in the closest thing to a town square in Ganges.

With fashion and personal appearance as rough measures of professional and socioeconomic status, I decide to conduct an informal survey of Salt Spring's demographic: sturdy men with chin stubble, clad in heavy, construction overalls; aging hippies with steel gray ponytails and colorful, thrift-store ensembles; affluent retirees in expensive, rainproof casual wear; young moms with babies snuggled close to their breasts in bright-hued cloth slings; artistic types with an eclectic, layered look and handcrafted jewelry; and a hybrid who defies categorization with his grubby, poverty-line apparel and an expensive laptop strung over his shoulder. I observe a smattering of smart-dressed professionals and the sole person in a suit is clearly a bank manager. To the list of overdressed, uptight, urban specimens, I can only add myself.

One savory bowl of seafood chowder and an hour of people watching later, two women walk through the door arm-in-arm and set my nose alarm to high-alert status. They order herbal tea and morning glory muffins before sliding into the seats beside my stool. The rest of Barb's friendly ambiance and entertaining assortment of characters fade away as my whole focus narrows to the tiny bubble of space that joins me to these women. My heart thumps wildly and my skin feels feverish, not unlike that delicious moment before your lips touch those of a new lover.

The tall, dark one, with a slinky length of black hair and an aristocratic, delicate-boned profile, I name Raven in honor of her sleek beauty and sultry, ebony dress. The other, older with thick, blonde hair and striking, violet blue eyes, I call Red for her stunning, tailored-fitted, crimson cloak, with a tall collar and flared cuffs — a kind of elven urban wear, the likes of which I've never seen before.

"So, you want to do the story of Inanna's visit to Ereshkigal in the Underworld for tonight's Winter Solstice ritual?" Red says.

"Mmmhmmm," replies Raven, looking over the top of her cup with a glint of mischief twinkling in her chestnut eyes.

"And one of us has to take off our clothes?" Red adds, laughing at some secret joke they obviously share.

"Well Inanna has to strip off a layer at each of the seven gates," Raven says, "but I think Ereshkigal should be skyclad as well."

"Have you sent an open invitation to the pagan community or only to coven?" Red asks, breaking off a piece of her muffin, "I want to know how big a crowd to expect before I sign up for skyclad priestess duty."

Oh my God! These beauties are witches — real, live pagans! I've heard that Wicca is common fare on the West Coast, and probably in my part of the world as well, I've just never met a witch before. My nose is twitching so bad, I'm worried I'm going to sneeze.

"This is a community ritual," Raven says, "The e-mail went out on Friday and I've had about twenty yes responses. Annie and Kate have agreed to co-priestess, and you and I have the title roles of Inanna and Ereshkigal. Are you in?"

Without meaning to, I suddenly lean into their midst and blurt out, "I'm in!" and then back away just as quickly, my cheeks burning a bright shade of beet. To my relief, they both howl.

"Willing to go skyclad?" Raven says, putting down her teacup and turning to me.

"Skyclad?" I ask.

"Meaning you have to peel yourself out of that million-dollar outfit in front of a group of complete strangers," Red explains, laughing.

"Is that completely necessary?" I ask, tugging at the bottom of my jacket.

"Only for Inanna," Red replies. Then, catching Raven's eye, they both start laughing again so uproariously that I can't help but join in, even though the joke is beyond me.

Red's real name is Kayla and Raven's is Selena. They pull up an extra chair and insist that I join them. I quickly scan our surroundings to ensure that no one else is listening in on our boisterous conversation. A couple of tables over, a dad splits a cheese twist between his two sons, both squabbling over who gets the bigger piece. Next to us a young woman, with a glorious abundance of mahogany, curly hair, bends over her laptop, clearly lost to the rest of the world. No one looks our way nor appears remotely interested in our little group.

I exhale long and slow, clear my throat and then spill my guts, sharing the whole story that landed me in their laps: the hunger that rose up from my soul, my encounter with the raven, the dream about the feathers, the bizarre synchronicities that led to my impetuous decision to come to Salt Spring, and my treasure hunt that guided me to Barb's. In a rare admission of personal stupidity, I even tell them about my overpacking and lack of suitable footwear. The words flood out of me and I don't let myself stop, or breathe much, until I am done.

Is this what it's like to go skyclad — peeling off the layers I wear in public to shield my private life from prying eyes? I have bared my inner sanctum to these intriguing strangers, leaving myself naked and exposed. But it feels good. My whole body is soft, and oddly empty and pliable.

For a few breaths, no one says a word or moves. Kayla's and Selena's teacups sit untouched and cooling in the middle of the table. Then Kayla gently turns my face so I'm looking directly into her probing eyes. I sense that she is checking me out, not in an invasive way, but similar in feel to my own scent-based intuitive abilities.

"Have you ever done ritual before?" she asks.

"No," I say, "The only witches I've seen are in Hollywood movies, and I'm thinking the remake of Bewitched is not a fair representation."

"You're right," Kayla says with a quick smile, and then continues, her voice slipping into a richer octave, "Something is shifting in you, Sarah. Your hunger comes from your disconnect from who you most deeply, truly are, and you are choosing to wake up and reclaim what is missing from your life. These inner shifts called the raven to your window and to your dreams. The raven is a bird of magic and transformation, and the Winter Solstice is its time of greatest power, so it's no mistake that you've found your way to tonight's ritual."

"What will happen at the ritual?" I ask.

"We will be enacting an ancient Sumerian myth," Selena says, "The tale speaks of the Goddess Inanna's descent to the Underworld, the realm of Her sister, the Dark Goddess Ereshkigal. The Winter Solstice amplifies the power of this story. It calls us to open to death of the life that we know so something new can be reborn within us. If you do this magic with us, you may be setting yourself on a path that will change your life forever."

"Are you still in?" Kayla asks.

I pause and consider what Kayla and Selena have shared with me. My heart is still beating wildly and I squirm restlessly on my chair. Their words are big, foreign, scary, enthralling, and I only vaguely understand what they're talking about. Oh my God — am I really crazy enough to consider this? Yes, damn it — be bold, be brave! If I don't embrace the mystery I find along the way and take some risks, then why the hell am I here at all? Kayla is right. Something has awoken in me and it won't go back to sleep. And I don't want it to. If this is magic, bring it on and screw the consequences.

"Can I keep my clothes on?" I ask.

"Sure, as long as we don't need a last minute substitute for Inanna," Kayla replies with a grin.

"I'm in then!" I say, and see my delight mirrored in their shining eyes.

I dig around in the closet and dresser drawers, tossing wardrobe options onto the off-white linen duvet. What was

I thinking when I packed all this stuff — business casual for an executive retreat in Seattle? And what am I going to wear tonight? There's not a stitch of black or red velvet or whatever else is appropriate for this kind of thing. Why didn't I ask Kayla to borrow something?

My neat room is now a disaster and I plunk myself down on the tangled heap of clothing. Am I in? Did I really say yes to that question? Yes to gallivanting off into the woods to a complete stranger's house — a witch at that — for a Winter Solstice ritual? A ritual — magic — hocus pocus — where at least one person is going to end up naked!

My hands shake as I grab a dark red tank top and a black yoga jacket and matching pants from the bottom of the pile. I pull them on and stand in front of the oversized bathroom mirror. This is the best I can come up with? Really?

The pretty smells of my toiletries and cosmetics, nicely lined up on the bathroom counter, shift my attention. Right — makeup — what about makeup? I don't think Selena and Kayla even wore mascara, let alone blush or lipstick, but I'm sure I saw black nail polish on one of them. Oh great — black nail polish — I wouldn't be caught dead wearing that!

I unzip my makeup bag; the mingled, floral scents and pleasing colors are familiar, soothing. With smooth brush-strokes and steady concentration, I apply a muted palette of earth tones to my eyelids and then, with the same patience and precision, I move on to blush, mascara and lipstick. Then I paint my nails a rich, vibrant red that matches my lips.

This particular crimson hue speaks to me as I layer another shimmering coat onto my nails. I envisage it as the color of the beating heart of the Goddess that Kayla and Selena spoke of earlier, sending Her life-giving blood into the world as the beauty that is so abundant on this jewel of an island. I sense a matching, enervated throb, rhythmic and deep, pulsing both inside and outside of me at the same time. With each pulse, I feel myself open and connect to something bigger, wilder and richer than my little mind and little life.

The mirror reflects back the beauty of my own face and I picture myself as the child, the daughter, of this grander force — a rosebud ready to blossom into a fuller, lovelier expression of myself. This thought, like the tender touch of a loving hand, shifts my lips from a frown to a soft smile. And then I start to laugh, a quiet, intense sound, with maybe a touch of hysteria. What's the worst that can happen tonight? No one is going to kill me, and it certainly isn't going to be dull. And maybe, just maybe, I'll find the treasure I'm seeking and answers to whatever is driving this adventure and my gnawing hunger.

I nibble on the salad greens and seed bun that I bought at Barb's. My stomach is flip-flopping too much for the Hastings House's gourmet offerings, and Kayla mentioned that there will be a post-ritual potluck. After a few bites, I lie down on the couch and doze off, the jetlag finally catching up with me. I wake up, with a start, to the crunch of footsteps on the gravel path outside my door. My watch reads a little after 6:30; that must be Kayla arriving to take me to Selena's house which is a little south of Ganges.

My stomach is still doing its muscular gymnastics as I pull on my warmest coat and set out into the clear, starlit night. The full moon, just beginning to rise, basks Kayla in a pool of liquid silver. She gathers me into a big hug.

"Excited?" she asks.

"Terrified!" I say, and we both laugh.

Kayla drives a new-model Toyota Prius, a sandy beige under its dusty coat.

"Jump in," Kayla says, "We're running a bit late. But given

that most pagans operate on Salt Spring time, we'll probably be the first to arrive."

"Fine eco-broom you've got. I didn't know they came with leather upholstery," I say.

"Only the best for us green witches," she says.

I barely fasten my seatbelt before my belly starts to grumble, stimulated, I'm sure, by the savory aroma coming from the backseat.

"I smell vegetarian stew," I say, "With leeks, tomatoes, eggplant, chickpeas, garlic, cilantro, a touch of cumin, and carrots and onions, a bit on the burnt side."

"Very impressive," Kayla says, "Add in salt and pepper and you've divined my recipe, minus the burnt part. Selena called for some last minute planning and distracted me from my cooking. What else can you do with your psychic scent?"

"Suss out good business investments, weed out unworthy suitors and stumble upon cinnamon twists and wild witches, as I found out today," I say.

"Aha! You've got a wild streak underneath that glossy exterior," Kayla says as she starts the engine, "But I'd already figured that out."

As Kayla pulls onto the main road, mostly empty except for a couple of vehicles traveling in the opposite direction, I broach a topic that I've been wondering about since I left Selena and Kayla to their ritual planning at Barb's.

"If you don't mind me asking, what do you do for a living?" I say, "Salt Spring's economy seems to be mostly tourism based, and you don't strike me as a bed and breakfast or artisan type."

"My husband David and I run a consulting firm, specializing in organizational change," Kayla says, "It's challenging to live here with this line of work, but we want to raise our son Josh in an alternative, rural community. So I have to travel a fair bit, but I can also do a lot of my work from our home office."

Then Kayla adds in a mock whisper, "I'll let you in on a secret — I've got an MBA alter ego under this red cloak, and she's a bit of an overachieving workaholic."

"Really?" I say, intrigued that we share similar professional backgrounds and traits.

I twist in my seat to look for signs of this alter ego in Kayla. The new car, the polished appearance, the easy confidence and way with words — all are markers that I recognize from the smart, successful people in my corporate world. But as far as I know, none of them wear red cloaks and practice magic on the side.

"Really," Kayla says, not taking her eyes from the road, "I grew up in a small factory town, with no culture and certainly no spirituality. I had a lot of brains and drive, and I wanted to live in a big city, so I got an MBA and spent the next decade chained to my career. The flaw in my plan was this lifestyle was costing me my womanhood and my soul, and that's when I started to change and embrace my spirituality."

We have left the street lights of Ganges behind and now navigate a winding, two-lane road lit only by the bright moon and intermittent, oncoming headlights. Large stretches of forest line either side of the thoroughfare, casting giant-tree moon shadows across our route.

"You weren't always a witch?" I ask.

"That's an interesting question," Kayla says, "Yes — I believe I was always a witch, and that all of us come into this world with our power and magic intact. But I lost my true self somewhere along the way. The pain of that loss is what changed my life. I became what I call a person of power — someone who has the courage to step outside of the life that they know, and is not afraid to do whatever it takes to heal their soul."

"That's not how I usually think of power," I say, "In my job power is about money and influence, and who is the biggest bully. But that's not what you're talking about, is it?"

"No, not at all," Kayla says, "In feminist terms, what you're talking about is power over, which is our cultural model of power. What I'm referring to is personal power, or power within, that comes from your inner gifts and divinity. A person of power seeks out these lost parts of themselves and works to restore their inner power."

"Do I have to be a witch to become a person of power?" I ask.

"No," Kayla says, "Courage is much more important than a specific spiritual path because reclaiming the lost parts of our soul is no easy task. That said, magic and Wicca naturally draw on our inner power and are very potent for deep soul work. You'll see what I'm talking about in action tonight. This isn't going to be a corporate-boardroom display of power, but something quite the opposite. Real power doesn't come from what we do in the world, but from who we are inside."

We turn right onto Selena's road. The moonlight shines directly through the front windshield, painting half of Kayla's features luminescent silver, while the side away from me remains in shadow. A quiver trembles down my backbone; it's the witch, not the corporate Kayla, who is in this car with me. I sense a tingling, outward force rising from her body that pulses against my cool skin and coaxes my secret longings from the hidden recesses of my inner world. Whatever she's got, I want it bad. But it scares me. She scares me.

We come to a stop in front of Selena's home, a small, wooden building nestled into the hillside, with an expansive, moonlit view of the ocean and surrounding islands. A profound silence, as vast and fathomless as the night sky, infuses my center and strips me bare of everything except Kayla's words.

"Can this happen to me?" I ask, my words catching in my throat as a single tear escapes from the corner of my eye, "Can I find what I've lost, even if I have no idea what I'm looking for or why I'm here tonight?"

Kayla catches my tear on her fingertip and touches it to her heart, as if my liquid emotion is a precious offering.

"Nothing is lost that cannot be refound," she says in a voice infused with an otherworldly authority, "This is the Dark Goddess's promise to guide you back to your deepest self and soul. If you choose this, Sarah, so will it be."

CHAPTER 3

DARKEST NIGHT

Twenty or so people brush up against each other in the snug quarters of Selena's living room. The space is lit by an abundance of candles that cast dancing shadows on the sage walls. The furniture has been pushed into one corner and the fir floor is littered with multicolored cushions. From my vantage point, I can see into the kitchen; its counters are covered with potluck shares, from savories like Kayla's stew to sweets like gingerbread and brownies. My stomach rumbles loudly in response to the enticing aromas.

This is no polite cocktail mixer like I'm used to back home. Full-body hugs seem to be the standard greeting, and my clothes already carry the scents of a dozen perfect strangers: Kate and Annie, the other two priestesses; Phil, a chartered accountant; Cassandra, an environmental activist; Zoe, a graphic designer; Mark, an organic farmer; Shanna, a dental hygienist; and a few others whose names have already slipped from my memory.

I'm not sure what I expected, but this isn't it. The diversity surprises me, not only the mix of occupations, but the age range — from an early twenties crowd chatting with Selena by the kitchen door, to a gray-haired couple, the senior citizens at this gathering, already seated on cushions holding hands.

There are round, curvy women in assorted witchy-looking attire, a lean, wiry man in blue jeans and a flannel shirt who looks like he hasn't eaten a cookie since he was two, and Phil the accountant in neatly ironed khakis and a matching shirt.

After making one circuit of the room, I squeeze myself into the corner amongst the tucked-away furniture in the vain hope of avoiding further body contact. I nurse a mug of spiced apple cider. There are no alcohol or drugs, yet this is the most relaxed and welcoming crowd I've ever encountered. No one seems to have pegged me as the odd duck in the mix, with my stiff hugs and shallow attempts at conversation. I could have come dressed in a grain sack for all anyone would care. Nor does it appear to matter that I've never done ritual before. But still, I haven't felt this awkward since my high school dances, pressed up against a wall, both desperately wanting someone to ask me to slow dance and balking at the requisite physical intimacy.

Then there is the handsome man who arrived shortly after me, with long, dark lashes, sea green eyes, weather-tanned skin and black, curly hair. Now him I wouldn't mind hugging or slow dancing with. What is it about green-eyed men that gets my heart racing? If Matt spent more time in a kayak and less in the office, he could be this delicious man's older brother. As if on cue, he walks toward me with his right hand extended.

"Hi, I'm Will," he says, "I thought I'd try a more conventional greeting. You don't seem a big fan of Salt Spring's love customs."

"Sarah," I say, returning his handshake, "You're the only one who seems to have noticed that hugging isn't my preferred first point of contact. Are you from here?"

"No, I'm from Vancouver," he says, "I'm a high school biology teacher and I just started Christmas break. My friend Hal lives on Salt Spring. When he told me yesterday he was going to a Winter Solstice ritual, I jumped on a ferry first thing this morning and showed up on his doorstep, begging him to let me tag along. I've always wanted to go to a ritual, but never had the chance before. That's Hal over there, flirting with the redhead in the lime green tights."

"The redhead is Rose," I say, "She works at the local health food store and knows pretty well everyone here. She smells of sandalwood, especially her hair. I'm guessing she has a thing for incense."

I take a deep breath of the scent rising off Will's skin.

"You smell salty, like the sea," I say, "But with a nice touch of bergamot."

"Really?" Will says with a laugh, and then puts his hand to his nose and takes a loud sniff, "You know I do! I had an ocean swim at Beddis Beach before dinner. Mental, I know, but it's a tradition whenever I visit Salt Spring, no matter the time of year. The bergamot is my aftershave. Do you smell everyone you meet?"

"Usually, and especially when I'm nervous," I say.

God, what am I doing? I never share this kind of personal information with a guy.

"You don't look like the nervous type. Nor the smelling type," Will says, "I'd peg you as a city dweller, with a well-paying career and expensive taste in casual clothes."

"Right on most accounts," I say, "I'm not usually nervous, and I'm an executive in an investment firm in Toronto. But I am the smelling type; it's like a second sense that I've had since I was a child. Other than that one quirk, I'm pretty straight-up."

"Then what are you doing at a pagan ritual?" Will says with a wide grin.

But there's no time to respond to Will's question because Selena is waving her arms to get everyone's attention.

"We're ready to begin," she says, "Pull up a cushion and form a circle around the edge of the room."

With much bumping up against each other, we form more of a misshaped oval than a circle. Will sits on the cushion to my right, with our knees touching. An unmistakable flush of heat sparks where our bodies make contact. Selena and Kayla stand in the center of our group.

I take a few slow breaths, in and out through my nose, soothing the fluttery sensations in my belly. I sense a coiled tension in Will, a quivering anticipation in his straight-back, motionless form and his gaze that tracks Kayla's and Selena's every movement. Not only Will, but the whole room feels still and alert, like a collective held-breath waiting to see what will come next.

Selena starts by asking us to introduce ourselves and to say what brought us here this evening. Annie and Kate go first and then excuse themselves for their ritual preparations. The gray-haired man and woman, still clasping hands tightly, speak next, introducing themselves as Rob and Liz.

Then Liz continues, "Rob has been diagnosed with prostate cancer. We only found out on Friday and, to be honest, we're not coping that well. We thought about not coming tonight, but then decided that what we need most are the support of our community and a dose of Winter Solstice magic."

Nearby arms reach out to hug Rob and Liz, and I see several people wipe away tears. My chest muscles tighten and my breath contracts; Rob reminds me of Opa Kass, and Rob and Liz seem so much in love.

One by one people offer up their stories — some happy, some sad, some funny and all refreshingly candid. With every sharing, my hips and buttocks loosen and settle more comfortably on my pillow seat.

On my turn I pause, torn between a desire to be open and

frank, as the others have been, and my habitual guarding of private, personal information. I look around this warm, encouraging circle of faces, and a tingling spreads from my heart outward through the rest of my body, calming my jumpy nerves and insides.

I take a deep breath and say, "I'm new to Salt Spring and to ritual. And I want to thank you for making me feel welcome. This afternoon I discovered Selena, Kayla and cinnamon twists at Barb's — all equally delicious I might add. I listened in on their ritual planning and I guess I kind of invited myself."

Everyone laughs, then I continue, "Curiosity brought me here, and something else, stronger and more compelling than just curiosity. I'm hungry for something more, something deeper and richer to come into my life. I don't understand what I am looking for, or what to expect, but here I am."

Will squeezes my arm and heads nod in agreement, as if I have touched a commonchord, that all of us yearn for something more than the fare of our everyday existence.

"Welcome and big thanks for your open hearts," Selena says after the final person has shared, "What a great way to start our magic together. Our ritual is going to be a sacred drama, enacting a Sumerian myth written over four thousand years ago. In this story, Inanna, the Queen of Heaven and Earth, descends into the realm of Her sister Ereshkigal, the Queen of the Underworld. At this time of the Winter Solstice, this ancient myth guides us in the ways of the Dark Goddess and shows us what it takes to enter into the darkness, into death itself, in search of new beginnings."

"For the novices in the crowd," Kayla says, "We're going to follow a basic Wiccan structure of grounding using our breath, casting a circle to create a magical container for our ritual work, and then calling in the Goddesses we will be working with. Annie and Kate will be leading this part of the ritual, and there are lots of experienced people here. Just follow whoever is wearing black velvet and lots of chunky jewelry, but not Francis or Sage over there; they're a bit on the wild side."

The two named offenders, both big-hipped, busty women, grind their pelvises together and pretend to make out; the group erupts in cat calls and laughter.

"Thank you, Francis and Sage, for giving us our first magical demonstration of the evening," Selena says with a gracious bow in their direction, "Magic is like great sex. It can never be adequately explained in words — you've just got to do it. Magic is in our bodies; it's instinctual, part of our natural fire and juice. And the more we surrender and groove, the better it gets. There is no right or wrong here, only presence and power."

"To be clear," Kayla says, catching my eye and smiling, "Selena is speaking metaphorically. Sex is not part of our ritual work. You can keep your clothes on."

Ignoring Francis's and Sage's disappointed groans, Kayla continues, "After we create sacred space, Annie will start our drama as the narrator of the tale and will guide us as the story unfolds. Kate will be Neti, the chief gatekeeper of the Underworld. I have the honor of being Ereshkigal, and Selena will be our Inanna. Each of you will be invited to do your own descent journey work in Ereshkigal's realm, and together we will weave the transformative magic of the Winter Solstice."

A drum sounds from a dark corner — boom, boom, boom — its pace slow, solemn, like a death march. Annie steps from the shadows into the candle-lit center of our circle. Auburn curls cascade over the lily white of her exposed shoulders, and a clinging, red velvet dress evocatively highlights the fluid power of her lithe, dancer form. In the short span of time since she and Kate disappeared from the room, Annie has transformed from a blue-jeaned waif into a staggering loveliness. Her beauty strikes me as a rare thing, seeming to arise not so much from her fine-boned, pleasing features, but more from an inner presence, as if an ethereal spirit shines through her skin and lights up the room.

"Please stand and let us ground together," she says.

With her hands on her belly, Annie begins to breathe in a deliberate, entrancing rhythm, pushing air through her throat in a way that somehow amplifies the sound. The red fabric of Annie's dress accentuates the movements of her belly, rounding outward with her long, slow inhalations, and flattening inward with her leisurely exhalations.

I close my eyes and let the music of Annie's breathing fill me. My breath spontaneously responds in a sympathetic resonance — slow, slow in, my belly rounds outward — slow, slow out, my belly flattens. The rest of my body remains motionless. I hear my ritual companions join in, enriching and intensifying this shared pattern, and melting the boundaries that separate us. My breath becomes Annie's and my neighbor's, and their breaths become mine, until we are all breathing together in one sensuous, measured cadence.

"Relax and empty your mind of everything but the sounds and sensations of our joined breath. Slow, deep, steady," Annie says in a low, enchanting voice, "On every in-breath, feel the energy build and swell in your belly. On every out-breath, let this power spread through your whole body, from the tips of your toes to the top of your head, pushing out and emptying you of extraneous thoughts and concerns, and of physical pains and tensions. Allow your breath to cleanse and renew you, and ground you fully in the present moment. Only the sounds and movements of your breath matter — in and out, in and out."

Annie's suggestions seem to enter my body and take on a life of their own. My breath stokes my belly like a bellows, fanning an inner heat in my center, and building an intense energy that courses through my upper torso, head and arms, and through my midsection, hips and legs. My mind and body feel strangely open and empty, yet simultaneously buzzing, like live electrical wires.

"Now on the out-breath send that belly energy down through the bottom of your feet and into the earth, like roots of a tree digging deep, deep into the rich, loamy soil," Annie says, "And up through the palms of your hands, like branches reaching far, far into the starlit sky. Feel the full extension of your being and your true, holy nature, for we are each made of Heaven and Earth, and of light and matter."

From a hidden place inside of me, I naturally understand and respond to Annie's words, fueling my inner heat on every in-breath, and sending that buzzing aliveness coursing through my flesh and out of my body, earthward and skyward, on every out-breath. Over and over I repeat this process until I imagine myself anchored in and stretched between, like a shining silver cord, the very heart of the earth and the heart of the stars.

For a brief moment, a part of my mind drags me out of this experience. I feel its twitching presence as it attempts to block me from the surging power and intelligence of my very own body, and from the secret, emerging abilities that must come from my soul. Then the compelling, seductive tug of Annie's voice catches me once more and pulls me back into its flow.

"Let the powers of Heaven and Earth mix and mingle in you," Annie says, "Let them enervate and ground you, and call you to be fully present to our ritual magic. Let them fill you with the beauty and mystery that you are. Take what energy and grace you need to feel connected and anchored, and then come back to your center once more, to your breath, and the rising and falling of your belly. Know that everything you need for yourself and for our magic this Winter Solstice eve is here with us now."

A pregnant stillness fills the room, ripe with a resonant silence and simmering power that mute the chatter inside my head and the earlier, playful banter of our group. My eyes open and take in the visible trembling of my limbs and the increased brightness of the space, as if the energies I am running spill out of me and join those of my shining companions.

Annie sways in the middle of the room, moving her hands in circular motions, seeming to gather up our joined energies. She shifts to face one corner of the room and says, "We cast our magical circle starting in the North."

Then, with a widened stance and a fully extended right arm, Annie draws a large, encircled star in the air as she intones, "By the powers of North. Her living earth to our living flesh."

With sweeping hands, Annie turns in a clockwise direction, defining the outer, circular edge of our space with the power I sense flowing through her palms. At each of the directions, she stops and paints another encircled star, her voice ringing out,

"By the powers of East. Her pure air to our pure breath.

"By the powers of South. Her holy fire to our holy spirits.

"By the powers of West. Her sacred waters to our sacred blood."

And then she completes our circle's edge by returning to the North.

Everyone mirrors Annie, turning and extending their arms in sync with her practiced movements. I join in, feeling awkward at first, not knowing these specific words and actions, but the forces coursing through my arms and hands speak the language of this magic for me. By the time we return to the North, my body is grooving in unison with the pack and crackling, hot energy is flowing through my palms.

Our hands stretch to the sky as Annie sings out, "By the powers of the Cosmos above."

Then we reach to the ground as she says, "By the powers of the Earth below."

And we touch our own bodies as she finishes, "And by the powers of our Shining within. Our magic is woven and our circle is cast. We dream the Mysteries, as the Mysteries dream us. Together we turn the wheel of life and create the world anew. Let the dreaming begin. Blessed Be!"

Selena's earlier words, that you have to do magic to understand it, come back to me, along with Kayla's assertion that I would witness something far removed from corporate-boardroom power. They are both right. Nothing in my everyday existence could have prepared me for Annie's stunning display of power and group process, nor my own primal, instinctual response to her ritual directives. Yet, on some other level, I sense that I'm not so much engaged in something new, but remembering things I already know.

One hand on my belly and the other on my heart, I search inside myself for any sign of doubt or resistance. I find none. In their place, I sense a slack-jawed wonder not unlike my first experience of multiple orgasms, and, deeper still, the hungry rumblings of my desire reaching for these awakening parts of myself and the matching powers I feel in this room.

Annie beckons for us to take a seat and I return to my earlier cushion with Will again by my side. I sit with my legs tucked under me, my spine tall and my senses keenly attuned. I can no longer detect any resemblance between Will and Matt; Will has become something radically different from my waking world conception of men and maleness. His features have taken on a feral, keen expression and his body a pulsing, liquid virility that viscerally pushes against my own throbbing, hungry form. Everything about him is wide open and uncloaked, as if he would deny no part of himself to this ritual magic or to me.

"Inanna's and Ereshkigal's story comes to us from long, long ago," Annie says in her melodic priestess voice, "from a time in our human history when we worshipped the Goddess and honored Her with offerings of story, ritual and harvest. When the ways of She — of life, earth, body, creation and beauty — were held as sacred and holy, and when women were our leaders, priestesses and guides. This tale was physically chiseled in stone in the ancient days, and then lost through the turning of the fates, only to be found once more in these times of great change and great need.

"On this Winter Solstice eve, these Goddesses remind us that the brilliant light of a new dawn is born from the belly of the darkest night, and that rebirth is not possible without death. All of life, including each one of us, is beholden to these immutable laws. These things Inanna knows. Descent is not to be avoided but embraced because only through the ways of Ereshkigal and the Great Below can Inanna rise up in Her full powers as the Queen of Heaven and Earth.

"Inanna teaches us that only by our willingness to enter the mystery of our own darkest night, with whatever wounding and challenges it may hold, can we blossom into a fuller expression of our personal beauty. In our ritual tonight, we travel this ancient tale with Inanna as She turns away from Heaven and Earth toward the Underworld. And we turn our minds to the Great Below to find the seeds of our own wounding and beauty that call us to rebirth."

Kate slips into our group, dressed in a sleeveless, floor-length, black vest, and abruptly draws our attention to the other side of the room as she booms in a rich and commanding voice, "We call to you, Great Goddess, who speaks to us in the tongues of fruit and mold, vibrant flesh and rotting carcass, and brilliant sunlight and moon-draped shadows. We open to your ways of body, breath, sensuality and joy, and of decay, destruction, loss and suffering. We ask you to be with us tonight in your twin presences as Inanna, Queen of Heaven and Earth, and as Ereshkigal, Queen of the Underworld. Guide us as we enter your ancient tale of death and rebirth, and the mysteries of this Winter Solstice eve. Please be with us now!"

Selena and Kayla, completely transformed into Inanna and Ereshkigal, glide into our midst from the shadowed recesses of the room. I gasp, along with several of my companions, as a shiver runs down my spine and shimmies across my skin. My nose draws in long, full inhalations, with my mouth slightly open, as if to drink in the essences of these magnificent, otherworldly beings. Through a priestess process that I cannot even begin to fathom, they have become these ancient story characters, not only in their costuming, but also by an inner force that is unlike anything I've ever sensed or smelled before. Though I hold myself in check, I long to reach out my fingertips to touch and commune with them, living flesh to living flesh.

Selena as Inanna exudes a proud, regal bearing, shimmering with a vitality and personal power that I sense rising off her form, like heat waves from a desert sun. Her aristocratic features and statuesque beauty, stark and breathtaking, appear all the more poignant against the austere backdrop of an unadorned, white sheath of gauzy fabric and a curtain of black tresses down her bare back.

Kayla as Ereshkigal paces back and forth, her blonde hair

teased into an unruly mane, emanating a barely contained, feral power and a musky scent, like a wild cat ready to pounce. She wears a strip of leopard-print cloth tied around her small breasts, and a narrow, black skirt slit up the sides that reveal her muscled, bare legs and bangled ankles. A thick, silver torque of a snake biting its own tail rests on her collarbones, matching armbands encircle her biceps, and a silver circlet with a suspended obsidian teardrop crowns her brow.

Kate and Annie stand back to back in the center of our group, one facing Inanna and the other Ereshkigal.

Annie begins a chant, singing in a voice as sweet and pure as a lark greeting the rising sun, "Inanna, Ereshkigal. We must die to be reborn. Inanna, Ereshkigal. Help us birth the new dawn morn."

Kate adds a countermelody one octave lower, "Ereshkigal, Inanna. Queen of Death and Queen of Life. Ereshkigal, Inanna. Guide us through our darkest night."

Their bodies move in unison as they weave their voices, creating one song of invocation and welcome to these two Goddess Queens. Others pick up the simple words and tune, some singing Annie's refrain and some singing Kate's. My torso begins to sway, spiraling the melody upward through my bones and muscles and into my constricted throat, igniting its latent powers of reverence. My lips begin to form words and I join Kate's call to Ereshkigal and Inanna.

The energy of our song builds like a growing sea that crashes wave-like against the walls of this small room and then sweeps back over us. I lose track of myself and time, as if I have stepped awake into a dream. It takes me several minutes to realize that I'm no longer singing; the room has fallen silent, save for the quiet movements of the priestesses as they take their places within our circle.

With the rich timbre of a master storyteller, Annie says, "Inanna abandoned Heaven and Earth and turned Her mind to the Great Below. She chose to descend to the Underworld, to the realm of Her mighty sister Ereshkigal."

To Annie's right, at the far edge of the circle, Inanna waits motionless. She looks like a marble statue, with the fine lines of her cheekbones, nose and chin lightly brushed by soft, golden candlelight. Her dark brown eyes seem to be illuminated by a vast wisdom that I sense but cannot comprehend.

Directly across the circle, Kate stands guard before Ereshkigal. With her long vest removed, she wears only black tights and a crisscross of leopard fabric to cover her ample breasts and solid, hefty limbs. She is now Neti, the gatekeeper of the Underworld, an intimidating sentinel with legs wide, alert, expressionless features and a black staff at her side.

Ereshkigal lounges behind Neti on a chair loosely draped with black fabric. She scans the room with cold, blue eyes, as impenetrable as the obsidian stone hanging from Her crown.

Annie approaches Inanna with a woven basket filled with lovely objects and says, "Inanna clothed Herself in Her royal vestments and prepared Herself for Her journey."

One by one, Inanna adorns Herself with these lovely objects: a golden circlet, a necklace of blue stone beads, a delicately embroidered vest, a red velvet robe, a gold ring and a tall, wooden staff. As a final touch, She dabs the corners of Her eyes with a patchouli-scented oil; its pungent smell brings to mind chartreuse leaf buds, rutting deer and the wild, green fecundity of a forest in springtime.

Then Inanna turns in a slow circle, Her arms flung wide, and says, "You are my faithful companions. I am going to the Underworld, to the land of death. If I come to harm, you must save me. Do not foresake me or forget what I have asked of you."

My heart pulses in rapid, irregular beats as Inanna squares Her shoulders and walks a few paces toward Neti at the gates of the Underworld. I choke back a sob as a voice inside of me wails, "Don't go, Inanna, don't go!" But I know I can't stop Her; this story was chiseled in stone long ago and no one can prevent its inevitable conclusion.

With three resounding raps of Her staff on the wooden floor, Inanna cries out, "Open up the gate, Neti! It is I, Inanna, Queen of Heaven and Earth. I have come to visit my older sister Ereshkigal."

Neti moves in front of Inanna and says, "Stay where you are, Inanna. I must tell the Queen you are here and that you wish to enter Her realm."

Though Ereshkigal barely moves, Her body gives off an intense, radiating heat. She scowls and gnaws on Her lower lip as Neti delivers her report.

"My Queen, your sister Inanna waits outside the gates," Neti says, "She has come clad in full royal regalia and seeks an audience with you."

Long moments pass, my heart still mapping out its desperate pace, and then Ereshkigal speaks in a slow, danger-edged drawl, "Neti, you must fasten the seven gates to the Underworld. Let Inanna enter each door separately and then remove a piece of Her royal garments. If the Queen of Heaven and Earth wishes to stand before my throne, She must do so naked and laid low."

My fingernails dig into my thighs; I try to slow down my breath and to compose myself, assure myself that I am safe, and no one is going to strip me bare or harm me. But I cannot ignore the blistering power that rises from Ereshkigal and sets every fiber of my being on high alert. Somehow I know that She speaks to Neti about everyone in this room. We have all dared to knock on the door of Her realm this Winter Solstice evening, and to stand awaiting Her judgment on whether we will be granted entry. Though She has agreed to open Her gates to us, there is a price to be paid.

Neti returns to Inanna and allows Her to enter the first gate. As She steps through, Neti removes the golden circlet from Her brow.

Inanna asks, "What is this, Neti?"

Neti replies, "Hold your tongue, Inanna. The rites of the Underworld must be honored if you want to travel its ways."

A brittle edginess suffuses the room, charged with an electric tension that jangles my nerve endings. One by one, Inanna passes through the remaining six gates, and at each Neti removes a piece of Her royal vestments, stripping Her, at the last, of Her pristine, white dress. And at each gate, with each successive humiliation of Inanna, my stomach and shoulder muscles clench tighter and tighter.

Ereshkigal remains on Her throne, saying nothing but emanating a barely suppressed rage in the taut lines of Her posture, the twitching upturn of one corner of Her mouth and Her heavy, growling breaths. I don't know what angers Her, but I fear for Inanna. And I fear for myself.

Inanna, stripped bare and humbled, moves past Neti to stand before Ereshkigal. Though deprived of Her outer vestments of power and status, She doesn't appear the least bit afraid or vulnerable. An inner luminescence extends outward from Her form, seeming to shine all the brighter in the threatening gloom of the Great Below. I catch a faint scent of roses in bloom and that musk of patchouli, and I smile, softly, briefly, momentarily reassured of the good thing still waiting in the Great Above.

Ereshkigal rises from Her throne and prowls around Her

sister, sniffing the air with flared nostrils as if She too can smell the world Inanna has left behind. But unlike my joyful response, She erupts in a lethal fury. A low snarl curls from Her lips as Ereshkigal roughly grabs Inanna by the jaw and fixes Her with a deadly glare.

My hand reaches out, knowing intuitively what will come next, how this thing will end.

"No, please no," I whisper.

Ereshkigal strikes Inanna's face and pushes Her to the ground.

As if from a million miles away, I hear Annie, her voice ringing with anguish, "Ereshkigal struck Inanna dead and left Her corpse to rot."

For one shocked, empty-minded moment, I stare at Inanna's pale body, limp and lifeless on the cold, hard floor. Then I clamp my eyes shut, wrap my arms tight around my knees and close myself off from whatever is going on outside of me. What am I doing here? What is this madness? I've got to leave before that monster Ereshkigal turns on me!

I press my palms hard into my eye sockets, trying to push myself out of this ritual, magical reality and back to my normal, everyday sensibilities. But I am in too deep; I am awake in this story-drama world and compelled to see it through to its end. There is more to this tale, more that I am meant to experience and to remember. Whatever I am missing from my life is here in this room — the lost parts of me and my inner woman power — it's here, in these priestess women and ancient Goddesses — I can smell it, feel it, in the air around me.

But am I willing to follow Inanna's lead and be stripped bare of my worldly status and accomplishments — everything I've worked so hard to achieve? Or perhaps Ereshkigal's dictates go deeper, to my good looks, my health, my job and financial stability, and my Opa Kass. Oh no, God no, not Opa Kass! My insides lurch as I imagine him lying at my feet, curled up in a fetal position, naked, dead. No, no, not him, not my Opa! You can't take him from me! He's all that matters to me! The only person who really loves me! No, not him, Ereshkigal! I couldn't bear it! I couldn't!

Inanna's voice sounds from inside my head, "You must save me, Sarah, and you must save yourself. Do not give in to your fear. Do not fall for the false pictures it paints. Remember that I chose, of my own free will, to descend into the Underworld. Nothing was taken from me that I did not freely give. New beginnings wait for you in the belly of the dark, but you must choose to be present to this moment and see where it leads."

My whole body shakes uncontrollably as I uncurl my limbs, pull back my shoulders and lift my head into an upright position. With my eyes still closed, I breathe as Annie taught us at the beginning of the ritual. Slow, slow, in — I fill myself with the grounding, nourishing energies of earth and sky. Slow, slow, out — I empty myself of the terrifying image of Opa Kass. Just breathe, that's all that matters — slow in, slow out — slow in, slow out. The desperation recedes and I shift into a quiet place inside myself. I rest one hand on my heart and the other on my belly. What do I choose? Am I ready to turn my mind to the Great Below and to find out what waits for me in the belly of the dark? Am I willing to pay whatever price is necessary to find what I am looking for and to continue on this crazy adventure? Yes — for now at least, tonight — yes.

I open my eyes and take in Inanna's inert body — lovely, fragile, broken — and an involuntary cry bursts from my lips, "No, Inanna, no!"

"Inanna, Inanna!" Will sobs beside me.

"Come back to us, Inanna! Come back!" others wail.

The thunder of our cracking voices and harsh keening drives everything from my mind, tumbling me even deeper into this ritual experience. A chasm opens inside of me, a black, gaping emptiness, and I sense an ancient grief, wider and deeper by far than my personal past, and wider and deeper than the grief of everyone in this room. And I know, immediately, intuitively, that we have entered the tale itself. We have become Inanna's faithful companions, pouring out our lament for Her loss and beholden to Her command to save Her.

Ereshkigal joins us in our grief, hovering over Inanna, brushing back Her raven hair and soaking Her waxen face with a river of candlelit tears.

"Oh my sister, my sister!" She moans, cradling Inanna's head in Her lap, "Oh my heart, my heart! What has become of us? What has become of us? What has happened to our living earth and our wayward, mortal children? All the gifts and wonders we gave to them — squandered — broken — gone, gone, gone!"

And we moan and wail with Ereshkigal. Inanna is gone from our world. Ereshkigal is gone from our world. I did not grow up knowing their names, their beauty, their power. I did not grow up knowing my name, my beauty, my power. The womanhood I carry, the humanity I conceive, are but shadows, tinny mimicries, of their greatness.

Ereshkigal looks up, Her cheeks wet and shiny, and wipes away the clear fluids running from Her nose with Her bare arm. Her silence spreads through the space, broken only by an occasional sniffle and haggard sigh. Gently Ereshkigal lifts Inanna's head from Her lap and resumes Her throne. Then She turns Her deathly gaze, briefly, upon each of us. When it's my turn, though my limbs tremble and my breath comes in shallow gulps, I unflinchingly return Her glacial, probing stare.

"Who are you to cry and wail with me?" She asks us, Her voice once again strong and formidable, "You are not the Gods come to bring Inanna back to life. You are mortals, and I will grant you this gift of truth. By your hands Inanna's destruction has been forged and by your hands She will rise again.

"It was you who tore Inanna from my side — crowning Her Queen of Heaven and Earth — granting Her the royal vestments and reverence of the Great Mother — while you feared and vilified me and my mysteries of the Great Below. The solar realm eclipsed the moon, the light overrode the dark, and the whole, holy cycles from life to death to rebirth were torn asunder.

"And you did not stop there. Gods replaced Goddesses. The ways of men crushed the ways of women. Dominion and death overruled creation and the nurturance of life. I will not recount for you the litany of crimes that have erupted from these festering wounds, mortal against mortal, and against the good, green earth. Nor do I need to remind you of the grave peril these desecrations have wrought, and that you hover on the brink of destroying the web of life that sustains you and your planet home. For I have taken your measure and see that we drink from the same well of loss and despair."

As Ereshkigal speaks, unwanted images crowd my mind: the view from the floatplane of a dense, yellow bank of smog hovering over Vancouver's skyline, all the more ugly and unwholesome against the spectacular backdrop of snow-dusted mountains; a beggar crouched outside the Toronto Stock Exchange last Wednesday, dressed in a shabby, thin coat, smiling gratefully as I dropped a handful of coins into his outstretched, dirty hand; and the late November news footage of the most recent mega-hurricane, wreaking havoc on the eastern seaboard, tumbling and tearing up four-story buildings, ocean tankers and highways as if they were made of matchsticks and glue. I feel sick inside, dirty, contaminated, a guilty party in the hopeless mess we humans have made of the world, but with no idea how I can make a difference.

Ereshkigal's eyes shift in my direction and I feel Her inside my head, as if She is reading my thoughts.

"But there is hope," Ereshkigal continues, holding my gaze for a second, "And that hope rests with those courageous enough to turn their faces back to my life-serving ways. Tonight you have shown me your courage by journeying with Inanna into the depth of my realm and by daring a taste of my powers, my rage and my grief.

"In return I offer you a secret, a boon. The magic that can turn the tides of your destructive ways, and call Inanna and me back to the waking world, is woven from your wounding and your beauty. You cannot recover one without the other. The new dawn is born of the darkest night, and the blossoming of your beauty from the depth of your wounding. Tonight, together, we begin this work by creating a magic brew, the dirt of life, which will call our beloved Inanna from Her sleeping death back to our sides."

Kate places a blackened iron pot at Ereshkigal's feet, tips in a container of rich, brown earth, and then says, "By the powers of Her living earth."

Annie follows, stirring in a cup of water in a slow, clockwise motion, and then says, "By the powers of Her sacred waters."

A palpable force rises off this simple mixture of dirt and water. I sniff the air and reach my flat palms toward its power; it feels like old, old magic, as ancient and primal, perhaps, as the Dark Goddess Herself. I breathe it into my body, let it infuse my core and then give myself over to its mysteries.

Kate softly hums the bittersweet melody of our earlier song

to Inanna and Ereshkigal, while Annie speaks with a muted intensity and a slow, entrancing rhythm, "Close your eyes, still your thoughts, then turn your mind to the Great Below and its mysteries of death and rebirth. Open your heart to your deepest longings and let them guide you to the seeds of your wounding and your beauty, waiting to return from the darkness to the light on this Winter Solstice eve. With these seeds, we will brew our dirt of life magic and call Inanna back from Her death slumber, and you from yours."

A dream-like landscape appears in my inner vision when I close my eyes. An impenetrable dark surrounds me, alive and whispering with hidden forces that gently brush against my senses and raise goosebumps on my exposed skin. I can only see a couple of feet in front of me and the ground beneath me. With Annie's words to direct my actions, I open my heart and let my deepest longings bubble to the surface. Though I have no names for these mysterious, compelling energies, I feel them surging through my veins and reaching up and out of my flesh to permeate the surrounding blackness.

A path appears at my feet, hewn of glimmering, silver stones, like moonlight transformed into solid matter. The stones lead me forward, and I step as silently as I can so as not to disturb the sleeping beasts that I sense in the shadowed folds of this dream world. I'm not sure how long I travel for, only that I keep putting one foot in front of the other until my way is blocked by an impassable slab of black rock with a polished, reflective surface. My wide eyes stare back at me from this obsidian mirror, my pupils dilated with undisguised desire.

I place my lips against the cool, smooth rock and whisper, "Show me my beauty."

The reflection of my face dissolves and a woman appears, languidly stretching and rubbing her eyes, like a sleeping beauty awakening after a long enchantment. Golden light shines outward through her skin and spreads over the sable rock surface, like the rays of a new dawn dispelling the darksome grip of night. She wears a plain white gown, its silky folds billowing in an invisible wind; her wrists are adorned with spiral, snake bracelets, and a thin band of silver, embellished with an obsidian teardrop, encircles her brow. A faint breeze passes through the stone wall, carrying hints of wild roses, composting earth and sun-warmed meadow grass.

"Inanna," I cry out.

She turns to me and smiles.

"Sarah," she murmurs and reaches out a hand as if to touch me.

With a start, I realize that her hair is golden, not Inanna's raven black, and that I am gazing into my own sky blue eyes, but I don't recognize their depth of presence and power as a part of me.

"Sarah," she says again, spreading her arms wide to reveal my fully unfurled beauty, "Thou art Goddess."

I propel myself against the wall, attempting to leap through the stone and claim this vision of myself. But the wall transforms into a blank screen of slate gray concrete, and an urban stench of gas fumes and close-packed bodies replaces the rose scent of my Goddess-self vision.

"No, no, no!" I shriek, pounding the unrelenting barrier, "Come back! Come back!"

I pound and pound and pound, until, exhausted, I collapse to the ground weeping. I have found the seeds of my beauty and my wounding, and the source of my soul angst that has driven this adventure. I am Goddess; my lost feminine soul, vanquished from the flat, concrete matrix of my modern womanhood and the waking world, still resides within me. But

I have no idea how to get her, me, back.

With a sharp stab to my heart, the dream landscape dissolves and my eyes spring open. The others in the room have moved on to the next stage in the ritual.

Annie and Kate stand facing each other in the middle of the circle, joining their raised hands to create a living gate. Three people wait their turn to pass through the gate and stand before Ereshkigal's throne: a man and woman I haven't met, and Will. My temples throb as I join the line and I rub them absently with clammy palms.

In place of the steely, impersonal rage I expect, I sense an unfathomable sadness in Ereshkigal's clear blue eyes as Will stands before Her. Whispered words pass between them, a sharing, I imagine, of the seeds of beauty and wounding that Will has uncovered in his ritual work. Tears flow down his cheeks and soak the front of his shirt.

"Please forgive me, forgive me," he says as he drops to his knees and buries his face in Her lap.

The rest of the room is hushed. Ereshkigal gently strokes his hair and waits until his shoulders stop shaking and his breath evens out. Then She stands, pulls him to his feet and places the flat of Her palm against his heaving chest. A smile spreads from Her lips to his. She stirs the dirt of life mixture, now resting on a table beside Her throne, with a gnarled, wand-like piece of wood, and then paints a mud star on his forehead with Her fingertip.

"My heart rejoices that you have found your way home to me," She says, "Trust the beauty of your manhood and what is good and deep inside you. Your journey begins here. May many brothers follow in your wake."

Will doesn't say a word, but nods his head and releases a long, slow sigh. Then he bends and lays a hand on Inanna's slim, motionless body. Our eyes meet briefly as he straightens up, and he lightly brushes my arm as he passes by to resume his cushioned seat.

I am the last to bow before the Queen of the Underworld and dare to meet Her unblinking stare.

"What offerings do you bring to me, my daughter?" She gently asks me, "What seeds of beauty and wounding do you have to share?"

"My beauty," I whisper, "My beauty . . . I . . . I am Goddess."

"I am Goddess," I repeat, as if the words themselves can make this true, "But I have lost my way."

Then I look down as a red flush of shame and a slicing pain cut through me. My bottom lip quivers and I bite down hard, desperately trying to hold back the building sobs that threaten to suffocate me.

With a tender touch, Ereshkigal lifts my chin and says, "Nothing is lost that cannot be refound. You need only set your feet on the Dark Goddess's path and say yes."

A tremor rises from my bones and ripples through my muscles. These are Kayla's earlier words to me, infused now with Ereshkigal's immense power and presence. I once more meet Her gaze. This is no gentle Goddess. She is terrifying; a blaze smolders within the blackness of Her pupils that could easily reduce me to ashes. And yet, deeper still, I sense only love; not a Valentine, treacle-sweet love, but a fierce, tugging love, like an ocean that insistently calls me back to its life-sustaining waters.

"Yes," I say, "Yes, I will set my feet on the Dark Goddess's path and follow where it leads me."

Ereshkigal dips Her index finger into the blackened iron pot, whose earth and water hold our dirt of life magic, and stirs in a slow, clockwise direction.

"So it is chosen, so it will be," She says as She paints a warm, mud-smeared star on my brow.

The mark prickles, not painfully so, but enough to let me know that there is power in Her words that won't be washed away when the surface layer of mud is gone.

On impulse, I dip my finger into the pot, bend down to paint a star on Inanna's forehead and then softly kiss Her cold, ruby lips. I am only inches from Her face, my hair shielding our shared space from others, when Inanna's eyes burst open and Her quick smile stifles my gasp.

"So it is chosen, so it will be," She whispers into my listening ear and quick, beating heart.

I pull Inanna into my arms, her nude skin melding with my sweating body, and press my face into the caressing folds of her rose-scented hair. For a few precious seconds, that is all there is, this meeting and rocking of our bodies; we are suspended together in our own private bubble.

When I look up, it's Will's gaze that captures mine; for one still moment, Inanna and my private bubble extends to include him. His cheeks are still wet with tears, and I want to touch them, taste them and take them inside of me.

And then a rush of noise bursts our bubble with wild cries of, "Inanna! Inanna!"

Hands pull Inanna and me to our feet and into the many arms of a group hug.

Annie begins a seductive, bass beat on her drum and sings, "She changes everything She touches and everything She touches changes."

Others know the song and join Annie. Kate adds in a countermelody and verse, "Change us, touch us; touch us, change us."

I rock my hips, stripped down to my tank top and yoga

pants, letting the building energy of the song undulate through my bones and muscles. With dream-hooded eyes, I watch the music ripple through the group — Inanna, Ereshkigal, Kate, Annie, Will, Rose, Hal, Rob, Liz, every person in the room, even Al the accountant in his neatly pressed pants — the song's rhythmic spell catches us all, calling us to weave our voices and bodies as one expression of the liquid power moving through us. A kaleidoscope of enraptured faces, with mud-painted brows, pass me by; warm, moist flesh brushes up against warm, moist flesh, and I gather the scents of others on my body, like a lover with her beloveds.

As our heat and passion intensifies, so does Annie's drumming, pounding out a tempo that moves our bodies faster and faster, with dancers egging on drummer, and drummer egging on dancers. The song's lyrics drop away, and we utter, in gasps, just single words — touch, change, change, touch. My hips are no longer my own, nor my rushing blood. And then the words vanish, and there is only the insistent voice of the drum and my dancing out a power too big and too beautiful for my body to contain.

At the perfect, ripe moment, Ereshkigal and Inanna meld their voices into a single, resonant tone that seems to gather up the wild power we have generated and coalesce it into a single, white-hot beam of energy. The drum and our dancing bodies still as we join our voices in this single tone. Ereshkigal's hands reach skyward and Inanna's hands reach earthward. We mirror their actions, some following Inanna, and others, including myself, following Ereshkigal.

The hot beam of energy streams through the soles of my feet, up the center of my vibrating torso and out my fully extended arms and fingertips, like a live electric current seeking its grounding in the starlit sky. My lungs pump in and out, in large, whole-body breaths, as this wild, ecstatic power floods through me — building, building, building — reaching a shaking, humming peak — and then, in a collective moan of recognition, our magic is done. I drop to my knees and press my palms and brow to the ground, my mind empty and my body spent. A hand gently rubs the small of my back and I take in Will's scent of ocean and bergamot.

I hear Ereshkigal's throaty laughter and glance up to see Her embracing Inanna in the center of the room, their forms haloed in a bright, golden glow.

"Together we stirred the magic pot of our wounding and beauty," Ereshkigal says, "Together we charged the dirt of life that awoke Inanna from Her death sleep."

"And together we seeded our magic into the deep listening Cosmos and the waking Earth," Inanna says, "We dream the Mysteries, as the Mysteries dream us. Together we turn the wheel of life and create the world anew. So mote it be!"

"So mote it be!" I burst out.

"So mote it be," Will repeats, and then pulls me, hot and rapturous, into his strong, encircling arms.

CHAPTER 4

PERSON OF POWER

A jarring racket wrenches me from the comforting arms of a dreamless sleep and thrusts me into a predawn gloom that seeps through the darkened windows. I bolt upright in bed, momentarily disoriented by the unfamiliar setting and the scent of others on my bare skin. The bedside clock registers 5:45 in neon green numbers. My hand slams the alarm button, but the insistent ringing continues. Then I reach for the hotel phone.

"Sarah, I know it's really early on the West Coast," Jules says, after I mumble a groggy hello, "but I had to get a hold of you before work and I wasn't able to reach you on your cell phone or by e-mail yesterday."

In the background, I hear the urban din of honking horns and a murmuring throng of people.

"Where are you?" I ask, rubbing my puffy eyelids and wrapping the duvet tightly around my naked body.

"I'm walking the last couple of blocks to the office, freezing my butt off. It's snowing and there's a nasty wind chill whipping through these tall building," Jules says.

I know the scene well and imagine Jules navigating the icy, grimy sidewalks of Bay Street, bundled up in a hat, scarf and gloves, amidst a harried, rush-hour crowd.

"I didn't want anyone to overhear this conversation," Jules continues, "Marsha is up to no good, and I had to let you know as soon as possible. I hate that bitch! I've had it with her sneaky, bullshit games! She's gotten away with this crap for way, way too long!"

"Back up a bit," I say, suddenly wide awake with the receiver clutched in my fist, "What exactly is she up to?"

"I don't know the details yet," Jules says, "Yesterday afternoon she was in the boardroom with Matt and Trent. She came out about forty minutes later, looking all smug, and then she kept her admin assistant busy for the rest of the day. I managed to peak over his shoulder and he seemed to be reworking the organization chart. I'm guessing Marsha is finagling the reorganization you two have been working on. With you out of the office, that can't be good."

"She wouldn't dare," I say, though the band of tension across my forehead tells me otherwise, "There's no way she is that ballsy or stupid. Matt won't let her get away with it. Give me a second, I'll see if he left me any messages."

I put down the phone, pull on my flannel pajamas and grab a pair of thick wool socks to fend off the ice-cold currents coursing from the soles of my feet through the rest of my body. It takes me a few minutes to fire up my phone and check my voice messages and e-mails — nothing, not a word. What's going on? Matt has always covered my back, but where is he now?

"No message from Matt," I say, my voice hollow and flat, "What do you think I should do? Pack my bags and come home?"

Jules doesn't reply. The lull in the street noise tells me that she has likely stepped into the coffee bar next to our office building. And then I hear the familiar voice of our favorite barista, "That'll be $2.60, unless you've changed your mind about the cranberry-oat muffin, very delicious!"

I wait, my pacing shadow looming large on the pale yellow walls, and picture Jules stirring up her usual, a dark roast, no cream, one sugar.

After a short silence, she says, "I'm back — just getting my morning hit of caffeine from Bill — he sends his love. Did you hear anything from Matt?"

"Nothing," I say, "Maybe I should come back and see what's going on?"

"Absolutely not!" Jules says, "She'll think Matt tipped you off, and that she can jerk your chain and you'll come running. She's a nutcase, Sarah, and nutcases love that kind of power. Please don't give her the satisfaction. Promise me you'll stay on Salt Spring and not show your pretty face in the office until the new year. I mean it, Sarah, promise me."

"Okay, okay, I promise," I say, but regret it immediately. If I can't rely on Matt to fend off Marsha then who is going to look out for me while I'm off on this little West Coast escapade? How much damage can Marsha wreak in my absence?

"Look, I've got to go or I'll be late," Jules says, slightly out of breath, "Let me do some more digging and I'll report back. Check your e-mail at around 2:00, that'll be the end of my workday back here in the East. Okay?"

"Okay, thanks," I say as I sink down heavily on the tussled bedcovers, "Please be careful. I don't want you getting into trouble on my behalf."

"There's no one I'd rather get into trouble for," Jules says, and then signs off before I can change my mind.

I sit cross-legged in the dim circle of light from the bedside lamp, with the darkness pressing in on me from all sides. This can't be happening! I'm a goddamn partner now! Doesn't that buy me something? A little respect? A little distance between the Marshas of the world and their petty power games? Aren't I supposed to be making the rules now? Clearly Marsha is smarter at this power and politics stuff than I am.

And Trent, of course Trent, I'm sure he has got a hand in this! This stinks of his style: strike at your enemy's weak points. This merger is a powder keg, everyone knows it, and Steve's departure and my promotion have surely raised office tensions, especially for Marsha. It would take nothing to sign her up for whatever battle plan Trent has in mind for me. I just didn't expect him to start on me so quickly. If he can take down Steve, Matt's best friend and partner, what hope do I have of surviving? This can only end badly.

Not able to stay still, I rouse myself and switch on all the lights, even the outside one over the door. Crumpled patches of black and red fabric lie strewn across the floor where I carelessly cast them off the night before. I never throw my clothes on the ground. And I never wake up smelling of people I've just met. Well, not true, I did have that one-night stand in my second year of university after a stress-induced tequila binge. I didn't ever do that again. My skin crawls as the morning-after scene comes back to me: of a crushed party hat, stinking hangover and the reek of a man's dried sweat on my body.

But whatever happened last night, with a crowd of perfect strangers, was of a whole different measure of intimacy than that one youthful indiscretion. And no one even got naked, except Inanna. I run my fingers through my hair and over my chest and torso, feeling the traces of their lingering presences down through my pores and into the core of my body. All that dancing and touching, Will's embrace at the ritual end, it felt so delicious and natural, but now I'm not sure. I've never let anyone in that deep before, especially not a member of the opposite sex.

Get a grip! Jules's call this morning is the real world, not these wild, pagan antics. Marsha and Trent operate by the mean, hard power rules of everyday reality — the game that I'm used to and know how to navigate.

My hand reaches to the crumbling mud star painted on my forehead that marks the promise I made to Ereshkigal to follow where the Dark Goddess leads. I can still sense the warm, prickly strokes of Her fingertip and the hot brush of Her breath in my ear, "So it is chosen, so it will be."

What have I committed myself to? I'm only here for two more days and then I'm going home, with no Salt Spring community and no Kayla to help me navigate the Dark Goddess's path and become a person of power. What do these things even mean? Whatever I did in the ritual was a fluke; I haven't a clue about magic or priestess powers or Goddesses. Is Ereshkigal really going to hold me to a promise I made in the passion and pain of the moment?

Yes — there was power in the words that passed between us, a vow that can't be so easily broken.

A queasy feeling bubbles in my insides. There is a price to enter Ereshkigal's realm and to be granted an audience before Her throne; the ritual certainly drove that point home. Inanna was stripped naked and then killed. Maybe this is what the Marsha and Trent situation is about. Maybe the price I have to pay to follow the Dark Goddess is my career. And what else is She going to demand of me? How far down will She take me? Will I end up dead at Her feet like Inanna? And who will save me — kiss me back into the land of the living like I did for Inanna — because I have no idea how to save myself? Damn, damn, damn! How did I ever get sucked into something so crazy and so way, way out of my league?

Mechanically I pick up each piece of discarded clothing: my tank top, jacket, pants, socks, panties and bra. I fold them meticulously, even my underwear, and then place them in the section of my suitcase reserved for dirty garments. Like me, they too smell of the otherworldly realm of magic: sandalwood, patchouli, candle smoke and my own and others' juices of sweetness and sweat. I will not wear these again on this trip, and maybe never again.

Perhaps I'm making too much of this. So I went to a little ritual, got a little carried away — does that mean I now believe this stuff about Goddesses and unbreakable vows? I'm a chartered accountant, with an MBA, since when did I buy into this kind of storytelling nonsense? How can a mythic character, no matter how well played by Kayla, screw up my life?

I turn on the shower, as hot as I can handle, and stand under its steamy flow, hoping to thaw the icy blood coursing through my veins. Muddy droplets trickle to the tip of my nose and I stick out my tongue to take in some of their remaining magic before they wash down the drain. With palms cupped under my chin, I catch the brown liquid and press it against my frigid heart.

Fragments of the evening ritual flood through me: Annie's enchanting narration, Kate's formidable guardian stance, Ereshkigal's surprisingly gentle touch, Inanna's red-lipped kiss, and my raw hunger in the presence of my Goddess self.

Other images crowd my brain: Marsha's squat, sour face, smiling like a trumped-up toad for Matt and Trent, and then brimming with hate for me — a woman completely at home with dirty tricks and dirty gossip to undermine me, her female competition; and my mother's stunning, perfectly painted face, with her calculating smile and calculated responses, and the optimum blend of good looks and smarts to get what she wants — a woman on top of her game, but hollow inside, with no love for anyone or anything, not even me, her daughter and only child.

I don't want to turn out like my mother or Marsha, women enslaved by power rules that bring out the worst of their nature. I want the power I saw in those priestess women during the ritual and that I glimpsed, tasted, ever so briefly, in myself — untamed, scary, sumptuous, inside-out power. I want to be like Kayla, a woman who straddles the corporate world and the world of magic, with the ease and grace of a queen.

The caressing water cascades over the round curves of my breasts and down my flat belly, marking its passage in sparkling drops suspended in the dark blonde triangle of my sex and the heat rising from my insides.

My beauty, my lost treasure: I am Goddess. I felt that feminine power inside of me — radiant, unexpected and surprisingly familiar. Maybe I truly have a piece of the Goddess within me, and maybe I can find and reclaim her. But at what price: my career, my life as I know it, or something more precious still? Ereshkigal's eyes, Kayla's eyes — I saw the love in their depth, but also a smoldering, death-tinged fire; She changes everything She touches — but what kind of change? And will I survive it? Despite the heat of the shower, the chill in my blood returns.

The midday clouds sport a bruised-purple underbelly that threatens rain as I trek the short half-mile from the Hastings House to Ganges village. There are no sidewalks so I navigate a narrow, pebbly shoulder that separates me from a thin stream of traffic. The ocean dominates the view and appears out of sorts, with agitated whitecaps banging and slapping up against their neighbors.

I pull out my phone and flirt, yet again, with the idea of calling Matt. But as my thumbs hover over the keys, I still can't come up with a legitimate reason for the call. Instead, I replay the messages I missed when I turned off my phone during breakfast: Will confirming our date tonight at 6:00; Kayla inviting me to dinner tomorrow night and telling me to call if I need anything; a recorded reminder that my car is due for maintenance; but nothing from Matt. With a disgruntled snort, I shove my phone to the bottom of my purse.

My mother, though mostly negligent in her parenting duties, did impress on me that a stint of shopping can paint a silver lining in almost any dark cloud. My closets hide a wide assortment of anti-depressant impulse purchases: delicate sandals that chafe my toes, a blown-glass vase in a disturbing shade of red, an elaborate food processor that has yet to emerge from its box, to name a few. The purchases themselves don't matter as much as the not-so-cheap affirmation of the act itself — I shop therefore I am.

Based on the recommendation of the hotel reception desk, I'm off to the Christmas fair at Mahon Hall to wander through its wide assortment of local-artisan offerings. And then I'll investigate a bit more of the village. For tomorrow, I've arranged a car rental to explore the island. I'm following another of my mother's life teachings: why wallow in misery when you can escape in distraction?

My heart rate accelerates from my brisk walk and I feel myself settle back into my own skin for the first time since waking. I turn left onto the main road that travels through the heart of Ganges, and in a few minutes I'm standing in front of Mahon Hall, a heritage building decked out in butter yellow paint with white trim.

Carnelian red doors open into a large hall displaying a veritable candy store of the creative arts: weaving, painting, wood turning, sculpture, jewelry, photography, clothing, and that's just from a quick glance around the space. A lone cashier at the entrance, wearing a gorgeous necklace of azure and magenta glass beads, offers to answer any questions on the artists and then leaves me to wander at my leisure.

But the last thing I feel is leisurely. An insatiable, very familiar hunger arises from deep in my belly and trembles through my grasping hands. I make myself move slowly from table to table: delicately running my fingertips over lily white, zen-inspired dishware; bending to peer into a miniature gathering of felted, red-capped gnomes; and examining the artistry of a silver-gray orca constructed of recycled metal. Inside, my gluttonous "I want" urges are on overdrive. I want that green glass and black metal, primordial-sized dragonfly. I want that hand-crafted chef knife with the maple burl handle. I want a full set of those breathtaking, lily white dishes.

I stop dead in the middle of the room and drop my arms to my sides. For years I've been bringing home pretty bags full of pretty things. I already have enough art, clothing, kitchenware and stuff to last me a lifetime. And still I am hungry, always hungry, for more. What is it that I truly want? Truly need? My nerves feel jumpy and erratic and a sour taste coats the back of my throat. I don't know what I need or want. I just don't know. God, I can't do this today!

Reluctantly, I retrace my steps to the door, arranging my face in an apologetic smile for when I pass by the helpful cashier empty-handed. But then I notice a short flight of wide, wooden stairs ascending to a smaller, more intimate display area. Before I can stop myself, I head in that direction.

Stark black against a white linen tablecloth nests a life-sized flock of wooden ravens. Each one emanates a distinct personality, speaking through their playfully carved facial expressions and body postures. Like a magnet, I'm drawn to one dark beauty. With wings slightly spread and knees bent, she appears to be on the cusp of taking flight. I reach for her, descend the stairs and make my purchase.

With no particular destination in mind, I cross the street, holding on tight to my carefully packaged, raven companion. I enter the grassy expanse of a small park with the ocean on one side and a grocery store and parking lot on the other. The space is empty except for a lone seagull perched on the golden head of a sea-maiden statue. With a flick of its tail, it adds a white smear to the maiden's unruly locks.

My feet lead me to the weathered boardwalk that meanders alongside Ganges's waterfront. A salty, moist wind dampens my face and serenades me with a melancholy, clanking tune strummed on the sailboats' riggings. The slate gray sky, congealed into a cloak of mean-looking vapors, extends downward to the choppy, dark ocean. Gulls swoop and screech in the threatening shadow of an overhead bald eagle.

I walk a short distance and then stop to rest my elbows on the walkway railing; its surface is cracked and faded to a dull gray-brown from exposure to the unrelenting elements. My skull throbs and my stomach is hollow and aching. So much for a pleasurable shopping excursion! Who would have thought I could feel worse than when I left the Hastings House?

With eyes closed, I take five or six deep breaths and let the biting, cold air permeate my lungs. Blustery gusts carry faint odors from the far, forested shore to my sensitive nose, and I register the natural mildew and rot of composting vegetation. The smells trigger a long ago childhood memory. An image of a chubby, little hand appears in my mind's eye, clasping a bouquet of autumn leaves in bold splashes of scarlet, pumpkin orange and golden yellow, picked from the carpet of maple, oak and ash castoffs at my feet. No orderly piles of leaves to be carted off in black garbage bags for my Opa Kass.

"Why is your lawn so messy, Opa?" I asked, "The neighbors have raked their leaves up."

"Mother Nature is beautiful in all of her cycles," he said, "Why would I deny the good earth the lovely food held within these leaves for the sake of a tidy front yard?"

Everything in nature was beautiful to my Opa, from the yellow-on-yellow of a dandelion basking in the summer sun to the brown sludge of rotting fall leaves. Even the tufts of grass reaching through the cracks in the pavement elicited his admiration.

"Look, Sarah," he said one afternoon as I was playing hopscotch at a schoolyard near his home, "Under this hard, hard concrete, little seeds dig their roots into the brown soil and stretch their green arms to the sun. All around us Mother Nature gifts us with Her acts of beauty. Even a tiny blade of grass can remind us that life is lovely and good, and can make us feel better when we are hurt or sad."

A single tear slid down his wrinkled cheek that held, in its shining depth, secret hurts that I was too young to understand. But still, I brushed the wetness away and said, "You are my gift of beauty, Opa. Mother Nature must have made you especially to make me happy when I am sad."

The steady plunk, plunk of raindrops on my upturned face draw me out of my reveries and back into my stiff, shivering limbs and my lonely stance on Salt Spring's boardwalk. What would Opa Kass notice if he was here with me now?

With renewed vision, I take in the subtle shades of smoky

gray and mauve in the textured folds of the clouds. From the boat riggings, the staccato cries of a blue-crested bird ring out before it dives headlong, streaking downward like a feathered bullet, into the frothing waves. Close to shore, I spot schools of tiny, silver fish, flashing like bits of captured sunlight, and a large, blue-purple crab scuttling sideways between rocks festooned with starfish in hues of soft purple, pink and orange. My flared nostrils register the enticing scent of grilled meat. I turn my back on this raw, visceral display of beauty and smell my way to the nearest restaurant.

A few yards away from the boardwalk, the Tree House Cafe wraps itself around a grandmother plum tree that towers over enclosed outdoor booths, embellished with whimsical, driftwood flourishes. A small, cozy, wooden structure houses a kitchen, indoor eating area and coffee counter.

A young woman, with a ruby stud in the crease below her lips and a chestnut braid reaching to the small of her back, seats me at an indoor table and takes my order: a lamb-meatball stew and a pot of chamomile tea. Sitar music plays quietly over the speaker system, and the walls are covered with the smiling photos of local musicians who play under the stars on the outdoor stage in the summer months.

I curl my hands around a steaming cup of tea, drawing its warmth through my flesh and into my bones. My thoughts return to Opa Kass. As a child, I was always perfectly happy and satisfied in his company, not only in our nature adventures, but in everything we did together. I never had to do anything, be anything, for him to adore me — his sweet Sarah, one of Mother Nature's acts of beauty making, unique in all the Universe. My parents didn't love me that way, nor anyone else I've ever known, including myself.

No, that's not entirely true. "Who do you love, Sarah?"

Opa used to ask me when I was little. And I'd answer, "I love you, Opa Kass, with all my heart." "And who else?" he would prompt. "Me, I love me too!" I would invariably reply.

What happened to that little girl in me and her innocent self-love? And when did I lose the effortless contentment that I felt in Opa Kass's company?

My server's bright smile registers on my glazed-over vision. She tells me that my lunch will be up in a second and offers to refill my teapot with hot water. Two women come through the front door, discussing their children's Christmas concert in animated tones, and are ushered into an outer booth. I am alone in this inner sanctum, separate from the low hush of conversation emanating from beneath the elder plum tree. My lamb stew arrives, with meatballs nestled amongst orange chunks of butternut squash and dark burgundy kidney beans.

Halfway through my stew, with my spoon hovering mid-air, it hits me — thirteen, I was thirteen, freshly emerged from the gangly cocoon of puberty when things started to change with my Opa. My mother claimed my weekends as her domain and no longer shipped me off to my grandfather every Sunday. I basked in her attention and approval, and forgot all about my Opa Kass. She was also enamored with beauty, but only the outer veneer of physical beauty, usually mine.

"You definitely have the Ashby profile," my mother would often remark, "Fine nose, full lips and sculptured cheekbones, but you've also got your father's light blue eyes and thick, blonde hair. Lucky girl, you picked the best bits out of your gene pool." Then she would move on to my firm, athletic frame and just-so curviness of hips and breasts.

"Not too much, not too little," she'd say, as if sizing up a breeding mare.

When my grandmother was present during these assessments, she would cluck her tongue approvingly, and then join in the debate over the right color of blush to best suit my skin tone and whether pearls were appropriate for teenagers.

As a high-powered advertising executive, my mother knew firsthand the essential role of physical attractiveness in a woman's brand appeal. For the next three years, she spent a good portion of every weekend tutoring me in the fine arts of the discrete, socially appropriate packaging and presenting of my goods. Makeup, hair styling, fashion, jewelry, posture and body language all fell under her province, along with the joys of shopping and spa treatments as remedies for most any ailment.

My weekly visits with Opa Kass dwindled to one Sunday a month. And in my new love for womanly footwear and fashion, I forgot about the workings of Mother Nature. Opa Kass never said a thing, not a word of judgment or criticism. We just did different things together, like art museums and fancy restaurants of my choosing.

After my father died when I was sixteen, I stopped my Sunday visits altogether. I don't know why. Anger maybe that my father had never taken the time to get to know me, and never once told me he was proud of me? Humiliation that my mother soon afterwards tossed our weekends aside for the young-widow dating scene, discarding me as nonchalantly as she would an out-of-fashion suit jacket? Shame that I had done the very same thing to my Opa? Grief over all of this loss? I really don't know, except that in my high school years I truly became my father's daughter, blunting whatever pain I was feeling in my drive for high grades and a prestigious university placement. And I've been working like a dog ever since.

I even changed my surname from Ashby-Mueller, the mangled joining of my British-German lineage, to the more elegant Ashby because I thought it would look better on my business cards. I turned my back on Opa Kass, abandoning him after all the careful attention and nurturance he had given me. Several years later, when I moved him to Toronto with me and renewed our Sunday visits, his love was waiting for me as if we had never been apart.

Opa Kass no longer asks me who I love. If he did, he would be the only person on the list, except perhaps Jules, but not me. I don't know what it means to love myself anymore. The girl child who held me in such high, unconditional regard stopped breathing many, many years ago. Maybe that ritual stuff last evening isn't crazy, maybe I am. And maybe the kid in me knew a whole lot more about life and happiness than the grownup me ever will.

The delicate smell of jasmine perfume pulls me back into the present moment. My server is standing in front of me. With a start, I see my empty lunch dishes on her tray and sense my full belly. I barely remember tasting my lamb stew. She is speaking to me, but I haven't registered a word.

"What?" I ask as the sounds of the restaurant flood back in.

"I was wondering if you would like anything else," she repeats.

I glance at the clock over her left shoulder; it's 1:45, almost time for my e-mail check-in with Jules.

"No thanks," I say, "Just the bill."

A five minute walk through the center of town takes me to the Salt Spring Roasting Company, which apparently has the best internet access in Ganges. Inside my brain everything feels bunched up: my ritual experience, Jules's early morning phone call, my shopping debacle and these long-forgotten childhood memories. I place the flat of my palm against my forehead; my brow feels hot and cold at the same time.

After ordering an Americano and a coconut macaroon, I sit on a counter stool by a window that overlooks a couple of abandoned outside tables and a rain-slicked street. Furnished to encourage communal loitering, a chocolate brown couch rests against a far wall and small clusters of tables and chairs fill the rest of the space. The walls promote the coffee bar's fair-trade, organic products and feature the work of a local artist: sepia-hued sketches of faces in profile, with downturned lips and eyes clouded over with dark emotions. The place is mostly empty — three tables with single occupants and their laptops, and no one in my corner of the room.

I check my voicemail first; there is a return message from Kayla finalizing our dinner for tomorrow and again telling me to call if I need someone to talk to. We've been playing telephone tag and missing each others' calls. Perhaps I'm imagining it, but I detect a touch more concern in her voice than in her earlier message. Maybe she thinks I'm avoiding her. Maybe I am. Well, not Kayla, more the smoldering bit of Ereshkigal she carries — that part I'm not so sure about.

Then I pull up my e-mails and ignore everything except the expected message from Jules.

Her note is cryptic and sent from her personal address, "Nothing new to report. Have a plan. Call me on my cell."

There is still nothing from Matt.

Jules answers her phone on the second ring, "Sarah, hi, good timing, I just arrived at the yoga studio. We've got about fifteen minutes before class starts."

Strains of soothing instrumental music fill my ears and bring to mind the smell of fresh flowers and the white, unadorned walls of the yoga space.

"Your note said you didn't find out anything new," I say, moving over to the far stool as some new patrons walk in the door, "And I still haven't heard anything from Matt."

"He's been out of the office," Jules says, "So don't fret that one yet. Marsha worked the entire morning with her admin assistant. Then she went out to lunch with Trent. He came by to get her and she was all smiles and ass kissing, like usual. Those two are in cahoots for sure."

My mouth tightens into a grim line. The Marsha and Trent bit of news is no revelation, though it still gives my guts a nasty twist. It's Matt's silence that is really disturbing. He doesn't need to be in the office to contact me; he could have called or texted me from anywhere. What the hell is going on? Why is he meeting with Marsha and Trent without me there? And why did he push me to take a holiday? He must have known that my promotion would ruffle some dangerous feathers, especially the deadly duo of Marsha and Trent. Things just don't add up.

By the rustle of clothing on the other end of the line, I guess Jules must be changing into her yoga gear, most likely her favorite red outfit.

"You said in your note that you have a plan," I say, "Nothing too risky I hope."

"I don't give a shit about risk at this point," Jules says, banging a locker door shut, "I've been working for Lead Digital for three years. I've never really liked it and I've always despised Marsha. But her treatment of you has pushed me over the top. I went to see the Emilie Carr exhibit on Sunday afternoon. That woman had things right. She painted and lived on her own terms, and her canvases are wild and spectacular. I want to paint like that. I'm thinking it's about time to dispense with Plan A and give up the nice girl with a nice job routine. Maybe I'll go back to art school and do something I really want to do with my life."

Jules's bitter tone hangs in the air between us.

"God, Jules, have I pushed you to this?" I say, "Please don't let my problems screw up your life. Do what is right for yourself, not for me."

For a few seconds, I only hear Jules's breath, slow and even, like she is making an effort to find her equilibrium.

"Helping you is right for me," she says, her tone softening, "You know my family history. My dad was a real fiend after a few drinks. When he went off on his rampages, my sister and I hid in our room, blockading the door with our dresser, while my mom took the brunt of it. I never once acknowledged what happened to her, not even when her face was covered in bruises, not a word. It breaks my heart to know I can't change what happened. They're both dead, so I can't even say I'm sorry. But I can do something different this time. I can try to protect you, and if I take Marsha down a peg in the process, all the better."

Now it's my turn to be silent. I take a sip of my coffee; it's tepid and bitter and I push it away, along with my untouched macaroon.

"Okay, Jules, okay, let's do this," I say after a long pause, "So what's your plan?"

"I'm going back to the office at 8:30, after yoga and dinner," Jules says, "I'll snoop around Marsha's office. Her desk is always a disaster and she has no reason to expect espionage, so I'm hoping she's left a hardcopy lying around of this new organization chart and whatever else she is mucking around with."

"Are you sure?" I say, absently shredding my napkin into thin strips, "Maybe we should wait a few days and see if I hear anything from Matt. It isn't worth the risk."

"Marsha and Trent are banking on pushing this forward with you out of the picture, so waiting isn't a great idea," Jules says.

On the other end of the line, I hear the familiar voices of women from our yoga class.

Jules says, "It's Sarah. She's in British Columbia."

She must be holding her phone outward because I hear a loud chorus of: "Hi, Sarah!"; "Happy holidays!"; and, from a lone voice, "I hope you've got a raincoat."

Jules returns the phone to her ear and then says, "Look, Sarah, I can't live in the shadow of a bully anymore. I need to do this for my own sake, as much as for yours. You're my best friend, and best friends stick up for each other."

I have to push past a tightness in my throat to get my next words out, "Thanks, Jules. You have no idea how much this means to me. But please, please be cautious! Promise me that you'll leave if anyone is there. Okay?"

"Okay, I'll be careful, I promise," Jules says, "But don't worry. Nobody is going to be in the office that late just before Christmas. When do you want to check in next? Can I call you at your hotel room tonight?"

"Tonight won't work," I say, "How about early tomorrow morning on your way to work? I have a dinner date with a guy from Vancouver named Will. He smells like the ocean — very sexy!"

The thought of Will makes me shaky. He's like no man I've ever met before — educated, well-spoken, handsome — the things that I typically find attractive — and open, vulnerable and oh-so-wild-man hot — definitely unchartered and terrifying territory.

"A date! No way! You sure work fast," Jules says, "Shit! Class is about to start and I haven't even asked you about your travels. How is it going?"

"That's too long a story for right now," I say, and then look up to make sure no one is within listening range. The crowd has shifted slightly since I arrived: still mostly empty tables, two men who seem to be having a heated debate on the couch and a handful of people waiting to order coffee at the counter. In a lowered voice I continue, "I went to a pagan Winter Solstice ritual and it seems to be jamming up my brain circuits. I'll fill you in when I get back over a nice bottle of wine and in the privacy of my living room."

"Wow, you sure know how to leave a person hanging," Jules says laughing, "I'll call you tomorrow morning at 5:45 and you at least have to tell me about your date. Try to have fun, despite this office bullshit."

I hang up the phone and stare blankly out the window as a dull ache pounds between my eyes. A few people scurry by, with heads down and collars turned up against the steady onslaught of wind and wet. A haze of drizzle blurs their edges and mutes everything to a bleak, washed-out palette. All the brightness seems squeezed out of my life: my promotion, my trip to Salt Spring, my treasure hunt, my magical experiences, Kayla, Will and my beautiful Goddess self. These are good things that should make me happy, but everything feels wrong, tangled, tainted, by Marsha, by Trent, and by me.

A new e-mail comes through on my phone from my Opa's senior home: "Sarah, this is Dr. Maddie Price from Sage Hill Manor. I have news about your grandfather's recent medical tests that I would like to discuss with you. I understand that you're out of town, and I was hoping you could call me tomorrow. I'm available between 9:30 and 10:00 if that works for you. Thanks."

I grip the edge of the counter, suddenly dizzy; the lamb stew churns in my belly. What medical tests? Opa Kass hasn't mentioned anything about medical tests to me.

A familiar face comes through the coffee bar's glass door

and I look down into Emilie's sparkling, hazel eyes.

"Are you okay, Sarah?" she says, squeezing my arm, "You don't look so well."

"I'm a bit sad," I say as tears well up in my eyes.

"Want a piece of my treasure," Emilie says, pulling a double strand of metallic blue beads from around her neck, "I found this on our treasure hunt yesterday — well, my dad found it, behind a big, big tree. We went on a walk up this huge hill and there were fairy doors in the rocks. Maybe the fairies knew I was coming and left me magic treasure. I've got another gold necklace. Can I have a bit of your treat?"

I hoist Emilie up on the stool beside me and she places the beads around my neck.

Ted and Beth seat themselves on neighboring stools and say hello. Emilie takes a large bite of macaroon.

"It's okay to be sad," she says, entwining her fingers in mine, "But even better to be happy. So maybe you should do something that would cheer you up."

"You're cheering me up," I say as my face breaks into its first, real smile of the day.

"That's good," she says, smiling back with a dab of coconut at the corner of her mouth, "But you need to make yourself happy because tomorrow I have to go to my granny's and grandpa's house. What did you like to do when you were a kid?"

"I liked to draw," I say, suddenly remembering that my prized, childhood possession was a purple silk bag that held my sketchbook and colored pencils. I never went anywhere without that bag. "Flowers, bugs, trees, anything in nature," I continue, "I used to draw with my grandpa."

"Well that's easy, they sell art stuff right across the street," Emilie says, slipping off her stool and tugging on my sleeve, "Come on."

Outside the restaurant window, the round, glowing face of the ascending moon casts a silvery trail on the still, black canvas of the ocean surface. Will sits across from me, candlelight softening the chiseled contours of his face and the laugh lines at the corners of his eyes. The smoothness of his skin and the smell of his bergamot aftershave tempt me to run a finger along the strong line of his jaw.

Our ritual encounter whetted my appetite, and I want more of this Will, more of his scent, his voice, his attention, his touch. Something feline and feral in me prowls around the edges of our shared space, like a panther in heat. I clasp my hands together under the table to keep them away from contact with his body. First-date protocol — I've got to stick to my first-date protocol — keep things surface and no physical contact.

My glance travels around the room as the server arrives with our bottle of wine, a local Pinot Gris. The décor is fresh and casual, with soft yellow and tangerine walls, funky, colored-glass and pale-wood partitions, and bright watercolor prints of island scenes. Romance is in the air, rising from the low, ambient murmurs of couples lost in private worlds of conversation. I catch Will staring at me, his head tilted slightly to one side and a faint smile on his lips; the heat between us rises up a notch.

"I'm celebrating," Will says, filling my wine glass, "My divorce came through today. I'm officially a free man."

"Free to do what?" I say, clinking my glass against his.

"You know, I'm not really sure," Will says, "But the timing seems pretty perfect, with the Winter Solstice magic, like one road has ended and a new one has opened up."

"Was the divorce your choice?" I say.

"No actually, she dumped me," he says, shaking his head, "She left me for one of the managers in her office, which shed a new light on all those late evening meetings. I was devastated when she moved out, but after about a month I actually felt better than I had in ages, like I suddenly could breathe more freely. I don't know how to explain it — it was as if I had been squeezing myself into the person that she wanted to be with, but wasn't really me."

"Regardless of it being for the better," I say, "it sounds like she put you through a whole lot of suffering."

"Sometimes suffering can be a good thing," he says, "My wife leaving me was incredibly painful, humiliating really, but I wouldn't have left our marriage on my own steam. I'm too loyal and too stubborn to give up once I'm committed. But without that pain and disruption, I wouldn't have gone to the Winter Solstice gathering or met you or done the many, many little and big things that are remaking my life for the better. That's what the ritual was about — beauty being born out of wounding — things having to die before something new can be born. Maybe that's why my divorce coming through today feels so right, like a good omen of sorts."

The smile on my face tightens as I force my muscles to stay in place. The call from Jules and the e-mail from the doctor at the senior home — they don't feel like good omens to me. My pain only seems to be promising more pain.

I take a long sip of my wine and try to push down my worries. Jules must be done by now and on her way home. God, I hope she is okay and no one caught her. And Opa, oh my Opa, what have you been hiding from me?

Our food arrives; we've both ordered a tuk tuk rice bowl. My panther-in-heat, chilled into docility by these unpleasant thoughts, has stopped her prowling. I change the subject to safer ground.

"Where exactly are we?" I ask.

"We're at the south end of the island in a little seaside village called Fulford," Will replies, "From Ganges you drive through the Fulford Valley to get here. It's very picturesque, with farmland bordered by a forested slope on one side. The harbor you see out these windows is at one end of the valley and Mount Maxwell is at the other. The village has become much more upscale in recent years. This place, Rock Salt, has had a complete makeover. It used to be a really grubby Mexican restaurant. I still remember a fly strip that hung from the ceiling by the food counter. It was so plastered with dead bugs that the living ones had free run of the place."

I poke my food with my fork and grimace.

Will laughs and says, "Sorry, not a great visual while we're eating. But, as you can see, the new owners have prettied things up, not a fly in sight and the food is much better."

Between spicy mouthfuls of chicken in masala sauce, Will and I cover a lot of ground. I carefully steer my side of the conversation away from my post-ritual traumas. I tell him about my Toronto life, where I work, live and what I like to do in my spare time. And then Will gets me talking about my childhood in New York, my visits to the Museum of Modern Art with my Opa Kass, and my precocious appreciation of the big abstract canvases of the modern masters.

"I would stand in front of a piece for a half hour, the only child in sight," I say, "I was mesmerized by the unrestrained, sensual dance of paint and painter in a Jackson Pollock work, and by Rothko's luminous world of color. My Opa always encouraged me and discussed the paintings with me as if my opinions mattered."

I lean ever closer to Will, our hands resting on the table, inches apart, but not yet touching. His gaze is intense, like nothing else in the world matters more than this candlelit moment.

"I didn't have that kind of culture as a kid," Will says, "The wild world, especially the ocean, was my playground. I started sailing with my dad when I was two years old. He would put his hand over mine and we'd work the tiller together. My parents divorced when I was ten, and my dad would take me for a month every summer, exploring the inner passage between the mainland and Vancouver Island.

"When I was fifteen, we returned to one of our favorite places, an unspoiled inlet that cut deep into the coastal mountains. The slopes were covered in dense forest and the wildlife was amazing: wolves, bears, cougars, otters, dolphins, eagles, ravens. On this visit, they'd clearcut one whole side of the inlet, right down to the waterline. We took our dingy over and wandered among the stumps. It was like a warzone, with the trees slaughtered and not a living creature in sight. It's the only time I'd ever seen my dad cry."

I don't know what to say. I've never experienced this kind of rugged beauty, nor its destruction. And my father never cried. Will is silent, lost in his own thoughts. I reach across those remaining inches separating us and take his warm, rough-skinned hand in mine. The panther in me begins to stir.

"They tried to do the same thing here on Salt Spring," he says, his eyes glistening with wetness, "A couple of business-men from Vancouver owned large tracts of forested land in the south end, including parts of the Fulford Valley and up around Mount Maxwell. They planned to clearcut the trees and then flip the land. But the local community fought them. People locked themselves to logging trucks, posed in a nude calendar, staged street theatre protests, made a documentary film, and harassed politicians, businessmen, the media and even the previous owner, a German princess — anything they could think of to protect what they loved. They managed to negotiate a deal before the place was completely decimated, but you can still see bald patches on the mountainsides in the Fulford Valley where they stripped the land bare."

Our server arrives to remove our dishes and offer dessert menus. We order apple crisp, key lime pie and mint tea.

"My apology; I didn't mean to go off on a downer tangent," Will says when we are alone again, "I've never been very good at small talk."

"Wish I could say that," I say, "It's what I'm best at — skimming the top layer and holding out on the deep stuff."

"Oh, I don't know about that," Will says, "I saw you during the ritual. You were fearless and you didn't hold back a thing."

My cheeks flush crimson, and I abruptly withdraw my hand and turn to look out the window.

"That wasn't the real me," I say, "I may be able to hold my own in a corporate boardroom, but I'm completely out of my league when it comes to ritual and magic."

I feel Will's unwavering focus upon me, but I continue to stare at the moon, now high in the night sky with its shining face partially obscured by a slow-moving, smoky haze.

"You were beautiful last night, powerful and beautiful," Will says, gently turning my face to take in his heart-melting, green eyes, "When you embraced Inanna something inside of me, the best part of my manhood, woke up. I know now that I have to change; I have to heal and become bigger."

Will's words push up against me, agitating the pressure that has been building in me all day, and rubbing me in places already raw and fragile.

"The world is in trouble, Sarah," he continues, "Clearcutting is only the tip of the iceberg. I've always lived close to the ocean and paid attention to her patterns and well-being. The oceans are dying; we are poisoning them and destroying precious ecosystems and species that we depend upon for survival. I've known these things for a long time, but I couldn't see how I could make a difference. I still don't really know how, but the ritual made me hopeful that we humans have better, beautiful instincts. And these instincts are connected to the Goddess, to women and to life. I am part of this change. How I think, love and act matter. You matter, Sarah. Inanna returned to life through your kiss. You have big, inner power; it's just been waiting for the opportunity to shine."

"I'm not beautiful and I'm not powerful, not like those priestess women," I say, feeling the color drain from my face, "Whatever happened in that ritual wasn't me. I had no idea what I was doing. I was out of control and following crazy impulses. I didn't think or care about what it all meant, or what cost I'd have to pay for my actions."

Then I close my mouth and clamp down on my words. My muscles tense up as I strain to contain the floodgates ready to burst open and wash me away. I don't want to lose it, not here, in front of Will, and in a busy restaurant filled with listening ears. But too many things are tumbling around and colliding with each other — disturbing thoughts and frightening possibilities — Will's scent and the hungry desire suspended in the space between us.

My mouth opens and the words spill out, "My job is falling apart. My Opa Kass is sick, maybe dying. I'm losing it. It's like someone is cracking me open and things are crawling out — bad memories and scary thoughts and big hungers I can't control. How can this make a difference, Will? How can blowing apart my life ever change anything or anyone else?"

Our desserts arrive and I don't want mine. My appetite and my attraction for Will, like everything else today, feels tangled and twisted up. I don't want to look at him or anyone around me. I want to go home, back to my hotel, back to Toronto, and forget this trip to Salt Spring.

Will asks the waitress to pack up our desserts and pays the bill. He helps me put on my coat and then ushers me through the door.

Outside by the car, Will takes me in his arms, and I feel his wet tears on my forehead and his steady heart beating into mine.

"Sarah, you are beautiful," he whispers, "More beautiful and powerful than you can ever imagine."

Part of Will's certainty seeps into me and I let myself surrender and melt into his warm flesh. I sense, see, the concrete wall from my ritual vision inside of me. A gentle breeze, infused with the wild-rose scent of my Goddess self, slips through the concrete wall to brush against my skin and enter my core.

My heart and breath quicken. I wedge my knee between Will's legs and press up against him, as close as I can get. My lips seek out his, gently, and then with a passion that seems to rise up from the earth and overtake me.

"My Beloved, my Beloved," some voice inside of me, outside of me, coursing through me, whispers.

Will responds, one hand cupping my head and the other on my lower back, pushing his hips, his hard maleness, up against my open femaleness. That power, that wild electric current from the ritual, when earth reached for stars through the portal of my living body, rushes through me once more, shaking my limbs, widening my vistas, as Will's body thrums and pulses in resonance with mine. I hold this tension, riding it, reveling in it, as long as I can, until it rises to a peak, an intensity, that I cannot contain. With a guttural moan, my mouth open on the base of Will's throat, I orgasm, not as a single release, but in shuddering waves that rock every part of me.

And I hear, rising from Will, from me, and from the sighing earth, "She changes everything She touches and everything She touches changes."

I jump back, as if I've been burned, but Will doesn't let go of my arms. With a husky laugh, his breath ragged and heaving, he pulls me back into his embrace.

"What was that you said about skimming the top layer and holding out on the deep stuff?" he says, "If you're not a powerful woman, Sarah, I don't know who is."

CHAPTER 5

THE PAGAN EDGE

Orange flames glow in the gas fireplace of my sitting room, dancing a bit of life into the early morning stillness. I am up and wide awake, before the sun, before the wind, before the birds, before another living soul for miles around, or so it seems with me cocooned in such absolute silence.

No shower for me, the salt of Will's tears and his bergamot scent still linger in my hair and on my face. I slide my hand under my thick, black sweater and clutch Emilie's string of shiny blue beads, warmed by their closeness to my skin. These are my talismans, precious connections to my new friends that just might help me get through this wretched day.

I log on to my computer; its clock says 5:30. Jules will be calling soon. There is one new e-mail sent late last night, 11:35 eastern time, from Matt.

With a slight tremor, I click on the message, "Wanted to keep you in the loop, Sarah. Will discuss the attached note when you get back from your travels."

The attached note and its communication trail of previous e-mails are between Matt, Marsha and Trent. I've been left out of the picture.

The note is from Matt to Marsha, with a copy to Trent: "Marsha, thanks for your hard work. The draft organization chart and staff changes between the Techstar and Lead Digital teams look interesting. I'm out of the office for the next few days, but let's get together early next week to continue our discussion."

For some reason, Matt didn't see fit to send me the new organization chart and staff changes masterminded by Marsha. This, apparently, is to be left to my imagination.

I scroll down and next find a communication sent by Marsha to Matt and Trent: "Thanks for the excellent meeting yesterday. I think we are making real progress in finalizing our new organization structure for the new year. As you know, Sarah and I have been working hard on this project. The organization chart and reallocation of staff I've put together reflect the need to mix up the TechStar and Lead Digital teams to facilitate skill and knowledge transfer between the groups. With the recent changes in senior management, it's imperative that we move quickly to finalize our new teams and have them in place for a running start at the beginning of January. I look forward to meeting with you both in the near future."

At the bottom of the page, I find a communication from Trent to Matt and Marsha: "Matt, thanks for asking Marsha about the reorganization plans. I've been wondering about them too, especially since Steve's retirement. Why don't we meet Tuesday at 1:00 and Marsha can give us an update? Everyone's calendars are free and I've booked the boardroom."

I shove the computer away from me. Matt initiated this! Matt! He invited Marsha and Trent to play these games. Did they trick him into this somehow? Or is he not the man I've always thought him to be: savvy, considerate and definitely in my camp? Something is wrong here, very wrong!

Marsha isn't smarter than me at this power and politics stuff, she just has no problem lying through her teeth and presenting the totally insane as perfectly logical. Nowhere in our joint "hard work" did I ever support the notion of mixing up the two staff groups. On the contrary, this whole merger has been a disaster; we should leave bad enough alone and keep the TechStar and Lead Digital teams as far away from each other as possible. And the idea of pushing for an immediate implementation, without my input or approval, defies any sort of justification.

Except, in the end, who's on your side of the table trumps truth and logic every time. Clearly Trent and Marsha are in this back-to-back, no surprise there. But what about Matt — where is he in this? And what the hell is he up to, initiating this meeting without me and then sending me this woefully inadequate, maddening e-mail?

I rub the stress points on the back of my neck and then head to the bathroom for a couple of extra-strength Tylenol to fend off the building throb in my brain. Before I get there, a Skype call comes through on my laptop. I sit on the couch with my computer. The screen fills with Jules wearing a scarlet bathrobe and cradling a supersized, black coffee mug. In the background, I see the saffron walls of her kitchen and one corner of a Frida Kahlo print.

"I'm playing hooky," Jules says, then yawns, scowls and continues, "I couldn't stomach a Marsha encounter today. I was worried I'd rip her ugly head off and then kick Trent in the balls for good measure. And that might have blown my cover."

I laugh and the pain in my head intensifies.

"You don't look so good," Jules says, "Don't tell me your date was a bust on top of all this other crap."

"The date with Will was good — the best first kiss I've ever had by far," I say with a sly smile, and then laugh again at Jules's raised eyebrows.

My smile instantly evaporates as I continue, "I got an e-mail from Matt — not nice, not nice at all."

"Maybe we should compare notes," Jules says, straightening up and putting her coffee cup to one side, "Let's get the bad stuff out of the way and then you can tell me about that amazing kiss. I'm jealous; all I came home to was a hungry, grumpy cat. You go first. What did you find out from Matt?"

"Not much more than you've already told me," I say, massaging the tight muscles in my neck, "Matt forwarded me a note of his e-mail communications with Marsha and Trent. Marsha has put together a new organization chart and is pushing for an early January implementation. Obviously she wants to move forward without my input. She's suggesting staff exchanges between the TechStar and Lead Digital teams, which is not a good idea and not a plan I would support.

"Matt didn't forward the staff change list and organization chart, so I don't have the details. And I don't know what he's up to. He initiated the meeting, and I wasn't copied on any of the notes between the three of them. Strange politics — I can't figure it out — but Matt seems to be playing me and I don't like it. I don't trust what he's up to."

"He almost caught me in my spy act," Jules says, "He was coming out of the office at 8:30 when I was heading in. I came up with a lame excuse that I'd forgotten my phone, and then hoped like hell it wouldn't start ringing in my purse. He looked at me kind of weird, like he suspected something, but what could he say? Besides, he had a long-legged redhead on his arm who looked way too cozy for a business acquaintance."

My stomach lurches and my face morphs into what I imagine as a blank, stunned look.

"Don't tell me you're sweating Matt's dating scene on top of everything else," Jules says, shaking a finger at me, "Don't go there, Sarah. Think about the shit he's pulling right now, and that sexy Will guy, and it will pass."

Jules takes a quick gulp of coffee and then reaches for something off screen. A second later, she is waving sheets of paper in front of the screen.

"I got the goods," she says as a mischievous grin lights up her face, "Marsha did leave a copy of the organization chart and a list of the staff changes on her desk. I made copies and brought them home. They sure made for god-awful bedtime reading! She is definitely trading staff between the two teams and, from what I can tell, she's giving you the Lead Digital duds and Trent the TechStar overachievers. She has Brendon moving to Trent's investment analysis team, and I would have pegged him as your replacement."

"You're kidding," I say, bolting upright so quickly that I almost send my computer flying, "Matt was going to offer him my position in January. No one knew about this, only Matt, Steve and me. But maybe Matt has changed his mind, or Marsha has a better plan for my direct report."

"No, she has left that position open," Jules says, "Her notes say that someone will be hired in the new year. There is no one at Lead Digital qualified for your job. Plus it makes sense to leave you understaffed for awhile, and get you off to a bad start as a new partner."

It's all I can do to stay sitting on the couch. I want to move — do something — throw something. But here I am alone on the other side of the country, cut out of the picture, with Jules sneaking around on my behalf.

"So Marsha and Trent are setting me up for failure," I say, "First Steve and now me."

"What?" Jules says, "You didn't tell me about that bit."

"I can't share too much," I say, "It's Steve's private business, but I can tell you that working with Trent was stressing him out. He wasn't having fun anymore and he didn't need the money or the hassle, so he chose to retire early."

"Well you don't need the money or the hassle either," Jules says, her bright eyes holding mine with their ferocity, "This is your life, Sarah. You've got brains, great credentials and options. You could work anywhere you want, do anything you want. Why put up with all this bullshit? Marsha and Trent can only get away with this crap if you buy in and play along. And if Matt is selling you short, then maybe it's time to go play somewhere else. Why not find a more healthy and sane game where you get to make the rules?"

"I'm not sure things work that way," I say as a few tears slip from the corners of my eyes. I roughly wipe them away and feel the fight drain from me, "Did I ever tell you the story of my grandmother's Great Aunt Beatrice? She was the lone wild woman in my mother's line. She refused to behave as a well-brought-up British lady, and started to hang out with suffragettes instead of marrying the man her father chose for her. Her family declared her insane, locked her up in an asylum, and that was the end of Beatrice. My grandmother first told me this dismal tale when I was a little girl, probably to scare me to death, and still loves to warn me of the dangers of being an uppity woman. I'm not sure things have changed that much, at least not for me."

"You could be right," Jules says, still boring into me with her piercing gaze, "But that kind of thinking has done a whole lot of harm to the women in our families. So maybe it's time to try something different."

"There's a whole lot of different here on Salt Spring," I say, and then stand up and carry my computer to the window, thinking to show Jules the view. But darkness reigns; the outside world still sleeps, with no brush of the dawn light.

"It's wild and rugged here — an uppity woman's paradise," I continue, "I've met powerful women like you wouldn't believe — witches and priestesses — beautiful and scary women. They put on the Winter Solstice ritual I told you about. That's where I met Will. Maybe here a woman could step out of the game. But I don't live here."

"The raven and your dream guided you to Salt Spring," Jules says, "By the sounds of it, you've had mighty unusual experiences, including a kiss to beat all kisses. These things can't be random. Maybe you've got a bit of Great Aunt Beatrice in you, waking up and ready to try on some wildness."

Jules stretches her arms over her head, picks up her laptop and moves into her living room. A golden morning light spills through an off-screen window. She turns her face upwards and her smooth, pale skin and glossy, auburn tresses are bathed in a haloed radiance. Then she smiles a Mona Lisa smile, as if she and the sun share a secret.

For a moment, time stands still and a surge of delight rushes through me. Mother Nature gifts us with glimpses of beauty to make us happy when we are sad. I straighten my hunched shoulders and take a deep breath, drawing a bit of Jules's beauty and strength into my body. The tension in my neck and shoulders lessen.

"So what are you going to do?" Jules asks.

"I don't know exactly," I say, "But I'm not ready to let Marsha and Trent beat me yet. I could call Matt and find out what's going on, but I'm not up to that right now. My Opa Kass might be sick. I've got to call his doctor as soon as we're done. She wants to discuss the results of his recent medical tests, the ones that he forgot to mention to me."

"I'm so sorry! I sure hope he is okay," Jules says, "I better let you go. Call me as soon as you get back to Toronto and let me know how your Opa is doing. And I still want a full report on that kiss and your Salt Spring adventures. Don't forget you need a date for my New Year's party. Matt is off the list, so maybe Will is an option."

"Now that would be my style," I say, laughing despite the unrelenting pounding in my skull, "Inviting a near stranger to stay at my house, delectable though he may be, and then bringing him to one of your outrageous parties. What's the dinner theme this year? Bring a food that represents your deepest, most secret desire? Besides, we said our goodbyes last night and he's going back home to Vancouver this morning. I think I'll be coming solo."

My smile fades when Jules disappears from my screen. I reach for my phone and call Dr. Price. My heart is beating so loud and so fast that I'm sure the receptionist can hear it as she passes me through to the doctor's extension.

I stand up and start to pace the room. Please let Opa Kass be okay, please, please let him be okay.

"Hi, this is Dr. Price, how can I help you?" says a crisp, friendly voice.

"It's Sarah Ashby, Kass Mueller's granddaughter," I say, "You sent an e-mail asking me to call you this morning."

I picture Dr. Price in the sterile, white-walled examination room, with its stainless-steel shelves, gray industrial furniture and single, spotless window overlooking the parking lot. I don't know her well — we've only met once, shortly after Opa Kass arrived at Sage Hill Manor — but I like her. She's younger than I would expect, maybe in her late thirties, and prettier too, with dark brown hair cut in a stylish, short bob and large, gentle, brown eyes. And she is funny; on that first visit, she and Opa Kass were laughing within minutes, about the indignities of old age no less.

"Thanks for getting back to me, Sarah," Dr. Price says, "I'm sorry to disturb you when you're out of town, but there is urgency to this situation. Are you okay with discussing your grandfather's medical tests over the phone, or would you rather meet in person when you're back in Toronto?"

"The phone is fine," I answer, keeping my voice steady and calm when I really want to scream that nothing about this is fine, nothing at all.

"Your grandfather has been feeling a little under the weather — joint pains and tiredness, not that unusual at his age — but I gave him a thorough checkup, just in case," Dr. Price says, "I'm afraid the news isn't good."

I lean against the wall, my body stiffening, barely breathing. No, not my Opa Kass, you can't take my Opa from me.

"It looks like chronic leukemia, most likely a more advanced phase," Dr. Price continues. Then for a few seconds she is silent, save for a grating tap, tapping of a pen against her gray metal desk. Perhaps this is a strategic pause, allowing me time to compose myself and respond. But my mind is blank; nothing comes to me, not a coherent thought or word.

"You probably know that leukemia is a blood and bone disease where the bone marrow makes a lot of abnormal white blood cells," she says, "Chronic leukemia is more common in older patients. I want to send your grandfather to a specialist for further tests to confirm my diagnosis and to determine the best treatment strategy. But he is refusing to co-operate. He doesn't want any tests or treatments. I was hoping you could talk some sense into him."

I start pacing again, back and forth in front of the gas fireplace, taking deep breaths, willing myself not to cry.

"What is the prognosis?" I ask.

"I can't say definitively without additional tests," she says, "But probably not good. Your grandfather has had a lot of health challenges, and I'm not sure he's strong enough to fight this. That's why I'd like to get a treatment protocol happening as soon as possible."

"Does my Opa Kass know you're contacting me?" I ask in a flat monotone.

"Yes, but he kicked up quite a fuss," Dr. Price says with a quiet chuckle, and again that tap, tapping of the pen, "Your grandfather is most certainly spirited. He wanted to wait until after the holidays to tell you. But I told him that you had the right to know and to have input into possible treatment plans. He insisted that it is his body and no one is going to tell him what to do. He is as stubborn as they come, if you don't mind me saying so."

"No, you've pegged him right," I say, grinning despite the constricting pain in my chest, "I'll talk to him, but if he has given you a flat-out no, not even God could change his mind, let alone me. My Opa has always lived on his own terms, and he will die on his own terms as well."

When I hang up the phone, I collapse into a chair and immediately dial Opa Kass's room, not giving myself time to process this news and totally lose it.

"Sarah, sweet Sarah, hello," Opa Kass says, "How are you? How is your trip?"

"I'm fine. The trip is going well," I lie, biting my bottom lip to keep my voice steady, "But I hear you're not doing so well, and you didn't let me know you were having tests done. I would never have gone away and left you. Why didn't you tell me?"

I hear the bed creaking and a rustling of blankets. Opa Kass doesn't answer me right away, but takes a noisy sip of a drink, coughing a bit before banging a glass down on the bedside table.

"What is the point of worrying you, Sarah?" he says, "What are a few tests to an old man?"

"The doctor says you have leukemia, Opa," I say, my words coming out harsher and more accusing than I intend, "And that you're refusing to see a specialist or have treatment."

"So what of it?" he says with a mulish note that I know so well. I imagine the obstinate jut of his jaw and blazing defiance in his clear, sky blue eyes, so like my own and my father's. "I've had enough of doctors for ten lifetimes. I'm done with them. They can leave me in peace."

"But you're dying, Opa," I say, pulling my legs up close to my body and hugging my knees tight, my voice finally cracking, "I don't want you to die. I don't want you to leave me."

"Sarah, my little one," he says, his voice gentle, like a tender finger brushing my cheek, "In June I'll be eighty-five. I had a stroke three years ago. I'm already dying, Sarah. All of us are. Every day we get a bit older, a bit closer to the end. The leukemia just makes the inevitable more real. Dying isn't what matters, Sarah. It's living, every moment, as fully and as best as we can. So let's enjoy the time we have left together. That's what I want. No treatments. No fuss. No mourning."

"But you'll be gone, Opa," I say, my eyes and nose running freely, "You'll be gone and I'll never see you again."

"You can't escape pain or loss in this life. They help you know what matters most," he says, "My love for you matters most to me, and to see you happy and making beauty and joy with your life. Everything you need is inside of you, Sarah. You don't need me to tell you these things. You already know, deep inside, what matters most to you."

My Opa's words, his tone, sooth me and slow my beating heart and lessen its pain. I uncurl my body and wipe my hand across my dripping nose. For several breaths we are quiet, comfortably so, the physical distance between us meaning very little. Like my first morning on Salt Spring, I sense his bony, withered hand slip into mine, squeezing my fingers tight, and then his grip loosens and his touch is gone.

"It's time to let me go, Sarah. Your Oma is calling to me. She's been waiting these many years," he says, and I hear that note of longing that is always there when he talks about my Oma, his wife, dead when my dad was a young boy. And underneath this, I sense something new, unusual, for my Opa, a weariness, "I'm ready, Sarah, I'm ready. It's time for me to go."

"Will my father be waiting for you, Opa?" I ask, my voice small and faint.

"No, Sarah, I don't think so," he says, "Your father never really concerned himself with others. I taught him to be too independent and self-sufficient. If he is waiting for anyone, I don't know who it is — not your mother — but maybe you, Sarah, maybe you."

My fingers reach under my black sweater and fidget with my strand of beads.

"Will you wait for me, Opa Kass?" I say, not able to hide my little-girl longings.

"Always, Sarah, always," he says, "I will never leave you. Touch your heart and I will be there. And I'm not gone yet so I'm expecting a nice present from you on Saturday and lots of good stories about your trip to Salt Spring Island."

In my mind's eye, I see Opa Kass shake a gnarled finger at me, his face breaking into a lopsided grin. No doubt on Saturday he will don his ratty, old Santa hat and insist on leaving this unpleasantness behind.

"Chocolate, Opa, I'll bring you lots of dark chocolate," I say with a sniffling laugh, "And maybe a special surprise."

"But no more about tests and treatments," he says, obstinate once more.

"Okay, Opa, no more doctors," I say, "Just you and me until the end."

"You and me forever," he says.

And my heart opens wide, like a flower to the summer sun.

I open my eyes to a room lit by muted sunshine. My mouth is dry and pasty and my limbs are sprawled at odd, cramped angles. The world has woken up as I dozed on the couch. The noise of bustling activities slips under the doorsill: the agitated rustling of branches, the bickering strains of bird song, and the monotonous pounding of an ax working its way through a nearby woodpile.

But I want to go back to bed, pull the covers over my head and pretend none of these dreadful things are happening. My Opa Kass can't have leukemia. Marsha and Trent can't be trying to sabotage my career. Matt can't have turned his back on me. I can't have made these strange promises that are turning my life inside out: to the hunger of my soul, to a wayward raven and to a Goddess that I'm not even sure I believe in. What's real? What's fantasy? Or does any of this matter? Opa Kass is sick, dying. That's real, that matters. But there's nothing I can do about it. Not a damn thing.

With an extreme effort of will, I stand up, smooth out my crumpled jeans, walk to the bathroom and splash cold water on my face. I stare into the mirror; my skin is pale, my hair dishevelled and my eyes dull and red rimmed. What now? What do I do for the rest of my day? The rest of my life? The next ten minutes?

Hunger pangs gnaw at my belly and the smell of apples pulls me back into the sitting room. My dessert and mint tea from dinner sit on the coffee table. I open the takeout box and dig into the crumble topping and gooey, sugary filling, breaking off chunks with my fingers and washing them down with cold tea. Not enough. I'm still ravenous, and I can't stay locked up in this room the whole day with the four walls pressing in on me. I grab my coat, purse and the keys to the rental car that the front desk arranged for me yesterday, and make for the door.

The wooden raven catches my attention from a nearby end table, her wings unfurled and legs slightly bent, frozen in a moment of transition from inertia to flight. Beside her, my untouched art supplies lie in wait in a violet silk bag: a sketchbook, colored pencils and fine-tip markers. I run my fingers along the smooth surface of the fabric; Emilie guided me to this treasure in a store on one of Ganges's side streets after I told her about the purple bag I loved as a child. I reach for the bag, clutching it against my chest, and then depart.

Outside a blanket of fog enfolds me; its moist, heavy air brushes my cheeks with the musk of things close to the ground, like decaying leaves and damp moss. Mist twirls ballerina-like around my ankles and distorts my surroundings into an impressionistic landscape of soft-edged smudges of color and indistinct forms. As I follow the path toward the parking lot, I make out trees, the hotel reception building and the rental car, a navy Ford Explorer. This muted, dreamlike vision quickly evaporates within the car's boxy interior and with the revving of its engine.

Once behind the wheel, I want to drive and keep driving, somewhere, anywhere, and lose myself in this fog-addled reality. But I'm hungry and I know Opa Kass would expect more of me, more courage, more presence of mind. I stop at

Barb's for lunch — a bowl of soup, a cinnamon twist and a large coffee — though my mouth is working, my taste buds aren't. The people around me seem somber and preoccupied. I smile at no one, and no one smiles in return.

Back in the car, I travel south toward Fulford with the vague notion of visiting Mount Maxwell or Burgoyne Bay in the Fulford Valley and sketching ravens as a special gift for Opa Kass. Will pointed out these places as likely raven hangouts on our drive back to the hotel after dinner.

A sign on the outskirts of Ganges points the way to Mount Maxwell. I turn right onto a steep, winding road that soon leaves the civilized world of cedar-sided houses, telephone poles and paved roadways behind. I slow to a turtle's pace and tighten my grip on the steering wheel as my tires dig into the muddy, graveled surface and bump their way along the rutted, narrow track. Higher and higher I climb through smoky banks of fog, hemmed in on either side by a tangled, towering forest wilderness. The trees, nourished by copious amounts of rain, are evergreen giants with their upper branches lost from view. Some have trunks so wide that it would take three or four people joining arms to encircle their girth. Even the ferns are supersized, with thinning wisps of mist curling amongst their three-foot-high, rusty green fronds.

After about twenty minutes of grueling ascent, the dirt road reaches a dead end. I pull into an empty parking area, navigating a maze of rain-flooded potholes. This is Mount Maxwell Park, one of Will's favorite hiking and rock climbing spots, with twenty-five hundred acres of untamed rainforest and the largest stand of old growth trees on Salt Spring. The air is impossibly fresh, purified by the lungs of this unfettered, green-on-green world: the olive green of fir needles, the pastel green of overhanging lichen, the emerald carpet of spongy moss and the waxy, dark green of the undergrowth.

I feel a firm pressure on my back that pushes me in the opposite direction of the few human objects in my vicinity: a wooden outhouse, a couple of picnic tables and a steel-mesh fence next to the steep precipice. Where the pressure is coming from, I can't say — the shifting breeze, my restless grief or the Dark Goddess? I don't know what is real and not real anymore, and I don't care. I only want to keep moving.

Immense, rough-skinned trunks surround and herd me along an earthen trail. Leaf litter crunches under my boots as I navigate a treacherous, irregular terrain, crisscrossed with the serpentine humps of roots that come up for air and then dive back into the forest floor. Three turkey vultures, with saggy, red gullets that jiggle ominously, hunker down on a low-hanging bough and track my progress toward them.

Maybe I should be afraid, wandering alone in such daunting wildness, exposed and vulnerable to forces way beyond my comprehension or control, and indifferent to my fears and grief. But a driving force in my guts, in my animal flesh, has taken hold of me and propels me forward. And I comply, one footfall after another, as the vultures fly from branch to branch in my wake.

The fog has dissipated and a small clearing, ringed by a semi-circle of young fir trees, appears before me. I stop, sniff the air and my nose says, "Yes, this is the spot."

I seat myself on a flat rock close to the cliff's edge that descends two thousand feet to the valley below. A restless gust blows away the lingering strands of fog and a magnificent, panoramic view opens before me. Far below, the light green and golden yellow patchwork of farmland in the Fulford Valley gives way to an olive green, forested mountainside; beyond, the varied hues of blue sky and gray clouds cast themselves upon a vast expanse of dark green ocean, liberally sprinkled with shadow-clad islands; and, farther still, the edges mark themselves with the jagged outline of the silver-gray mountains of Vancouver Island and Washington State.

At first I only take in the splendor, but then I notice pieces of this picture that are discordant with the rest: ugly, rectangular slashes gouged here and there into the forested slopes across the valley. These must be the clearcuts that Will told me about at dinner.

I pull my violet bag from around my neck and take out my sketchbook and pencils. Although I stopped making art at thirteen, my pencils move across the page with surety, as if it's my hands, not my eyes, absorbing and drawing this scene. My fingers express the level of abstraction added by height and distance that blur the solid, distinct shapes of things and meld colors with their neighbors. I move quickly, my yellow and green pencils capturing the meandering course of gentle farmland through the valley core, and the black, gray and green hues of the coarse-textured forests rising up to a blue-gray sky. I reach for red — blood red, black-red, death colors — and slash the clearcuts onto my art.

My heart and chest muscles constrict, threatening to cut off my breath, but I do not close down this pain; I put it on the page. With every red stroke, I open myself wide to these gaping wounds on the body of the earth.

A wild wind rises from the valley floor, tangling my hair, wailing in the nearby branches. I hear Ereshkigal's voice moaning, "Oh my heart, my heart! My body, my body!"

And I am back in the Winter Solstice magic. The concrete wall from my ritual vision rises up before me. It becomes transparent and I see my Goddess self on the other side, curled up in the green grass in a shimmering white gown. Her chest slowly rises and falls as she sleeps and her red lips are slightly parted, as if ripe for my awakening kiss.

But no, I can't, I can't! If I wake her then Opa Kass will die. I will lose my job. I will lose my mind.

The concrete wall turns solid, impenetrable, transformed into a gravestone. I can't reach her, touch her or kiss her; she is lost to me. And I am on all fours, my head pressed hard against that frigid, unforgiving stone — wailing with the winds, wailing with Ereshkigal — lost between two worlds: my life as I know it and the life those ruby lips call me to.

Help me — someone, something — help me please!

To my left, an insistent cawing, three and then two calls repeating slowly, pulls me out of my Winter Solstice vision and back into the raw beauty of Mount Maxell. The rough surface of the lichen-stained rock digs into my knees and palms, and my sketchbook and red pencils lie scattered around me. A few feet away on the far corner of the rock, a sleek, midnight black raven watches me. Her feathers are smooth and unruffled, and she seems unperturbed by my human companionship. With her wings slightly spread, she bends her knees and then leaps into the air and over the precipice, catching an updraft from the valley below.

A quiver runs the length of my body, humming through my nerve endings and loosening the built-up tension in my shoulder blades and skull. Tiny, birdlike, jerking motions tilt my head from left to right and back again, as if to reorient the alignment of my brain with my backbone. The top of my spine opens up and a liquid-gold energy flows down my back to my root and branches off to fill my arms and legs. Like a magic potion, this energy seems to wake another kind of intelligence in my body. My vision alters, transforming into a wide-scope, avian seeing and sensing, and my nostrils begin to pulse in quick breaths that drink in the forest-infused drafts. With hooded eyes and a mischievous tilt to the corners of my mouth, I walk toward the cliff where the edge beckons me. I stop a few paces short of the plunging drop, plant my feet firmly on the flat ground, and then extend my torso forward and spread my arms wide, as if primed to soar into the sky.

Directly in front of me, my raven companion hovers, seemingly motionless in the updrafts, her feathers iridescent in the low-hanging sun. She speaks to me in a complex, guttural rattle that sends tremors through my shifting form. I close my eyes and let her raven-world sensibilities completely overtake me. My arms morph into ebony wings and my feathered torso undulates, slowly, rhythmically, in synch with the faintest shifts in the air flow. I am no longer human; I am raven, flying side-by-side with my black-feathered kin.

My attention is drawn inward to the fine-line balance of remaining suspended in place. The dense earth drags me downward as the unseen stars pull me to greater heights; they speak to me through the touch and tug of energy and air currents on feather; I answer in the nuanced movements of bone, sinew and flesh. Every nerve in my bird body sings a yes, yes, yes to this raw, elemental communion, and I open my beak in a piercing outpouring of raucous delight.

Again the raven speaks to me, a staccato toc-toc-toc, and somehow I know this is a goodbye, that our time together is drawing to a close. I feel myself start to descend as the force of gravity gains over the power of the stars. No, no, I don't want this to end! Please raven, let me stay with you, fly with you. I don't want to go back to my human form and the pain and grief waiting for me.

"Do not resist what must be," the wind whispers, "Take what you need in this moment. Let yourself be changed."

The wind enters my lungs and begins to breathe with me, wide and deep. My sensory awareness shifts to a still place within and below the physical immediacy of feather, muscle, bone and blood; a place where ravens dream between the worlds. With my raven dreambody, I sense the electric thrill and see the silver strands of light that connect me with all things: the drag of earth, the pull of sky and the dance of wind; the trees, the rocks and the warm- and cold-blooded forest creatures; the movements of moon, tide and deep-swimming salmon; the clearcuts on the mountainside and the dying ocean; and my motionless human form perched at the edge of the rock cliff.

Through this raven awareness, I see the silver strands of light that connect my human body to earth, sky, wind, trees, rocks, ocean, moon, salmon and forest creatures, and to the wounds of the living earth and her ocean waters. My pulsing light and my streaming blood are part of this greater, silver-threaded weaving of life. One world, one heart, one breath joins us all in our beauty and our wounding. My life and my humanity are big, complex, luminescent. I matter because I am.

As I sense myself losing altitude, tumbling downward and compressing back into the heaviness of my earth-bound human body, my perception shifts again. This time I witness a dreamlike vision of my raven companion. She flies through an open window into the study of my Toronto townhouse and makes a strutting circuit around the tidy room. Then she starts pulling open drawers with her beak, tossing out this and that, yanking things off of shelves and collecting pretty, shining bits and putting them carefully to one side. The raven looks in my direction, traps me in her gaze and then dips her head and takes flight.

My blue eyes snap open, shrunken back to their myopic,

human capacity. I am no longer a raven; I am Sarah once more. Dizzy and disoriented, I stumble backwards and run my fingertips over my features — no feathers, no beak — just me, little, disconnected me. My face crumples up as my body pushes out wracking sobs for a loss vaster than my Opa Kass, my job and my well-ordered life. There is a reality beyond that concrete wall where I can fly with ravens, where I live and breathe connected to all things, and where that lost part of me, my sleeping beauty, is awake and free. But this reality has vanished along with the raven and I have no idea how to get it back.

Every part of me aches and I'm frozen to the bone. I rub my eyes and take a look around. The dimming light tells me that twilight is fast approaching, and the dense fog has returned, limiting my visibility in every direction. The precipice is there, a yard or so in front of me, and I scramble back until I bump against the flat rock, with my purse and sketching materials littered around its perimeter. I quickly gather up my belongings, slipping my art supplies back into my silk bag, and then turn around in a full circle. I cannot see or smell anything familiar; the certainty that led me to this place is gone.

With my hands held out in front of me, squinting my eyes to cut through the fog, I turn away from the cliff's edge and start walking. I cower at the sound of the flapping wings of a large bird beyond my vision; maybe the vultures are on my trail once again. My heel catches on a jutting rock and I land sprawled on the ground, tearing my jeans at the knee and gouging a cut along my right wrist. Slowly I get back to my feet, keeping my damaged arm close to my side. The wind has picked up and seems to have changed directions, coming at me from my right side rather than from the cliffs at my back. I stop moving, frozen in place. I have no idea of the topography of this park.

What if there are other precipices close by? I'm lost, truly lost!

Nothing is lost that cannot be refound — Ereshkigal's words, Kayla's words. Kayla who I have avoided since the Winter Solstice ritual, frightened of the Dark Goddess powers she carries; Kayla who has let me into her world and offered me nothing but kindness and support; Kayla who knows this alternative world of magic and can help me find my way out of this mess I've gotten myself into. I pull out my cell phone and dial her number.

The phone rings three times and a breathless voice comes on the line, "Sarah, is that you? Where are you? I've had you on my mind all afternoon. Are you okay?"

I'm shaking so much that it's hard to get the words out, "I'm on Mount Maxwell. I came for a hike and got lost. It's fogged in and getting dark and I don't know how to get to my car."

"It's okay, don't worry," Kayla says, "I know Mount Maxwell. I've been up there in the dead of night doing ritual. Take a few deep breaths. You're going to be okay, I promise. I'll help you find your way to the path."

I take several slow, measured breaths.

"Thanks, Kayla," I say, "That's much better."

"I want you to hold the line for a second," Kayla says, "I have a friend who lives close to Mount Maxwell. I'll call him on my cell and ask him to meet you in the parking lot. He can drive you to my place if you need extra support."

I slump to the ground, my knees tucked up close for warmth.

Kayla soon returns on the line, her voice calm and soothing, "Tell me, as best you can, where you are."

I describe the trail that I followed and the flat area with the semi-circle of fir trees where I stopped.

"I know the spot," Kayla says, "I've done ritual with Selena in that exact location. Walk with the cliff to your back and you'll reach the path. Turn left, follow the trail, and you'll find the parking lot. Can you do that?"

"Yes, yes I think so," I reply.

Within a few yards, I reach the semi-circle of fir trees. The land starts to slope down and I veer slightly to the left. Though the fog shuts me in on all sides, the rocks and soil seem to reach up through my boots to guide and direct me. The open area gives way to dense forest and immediately I spot a narrow strip of brown earth winding between the looming trunks.

"I'm okay," I say, "I've found the path."

The phone is dead. Kayla is gone and I'm alone in the near dark.

The shadows and night noises gather around me: the nearby hoot of an owl, tiny patches of moving darkness that I guess to be bats, and the crunch of twigs and musky scent of a larger animal. I look down; whether by a trick of the fog and the fading light, or another mystery, the earth beneath my feet appears to shine. I let out my held breath and smile.

Step by step, the path leads me forward from the deepening gloom into a welcoming light. A car waits for me, the parking lot aglow with its headlights. The man behind the wheel is Oak, the star-tattooed cab driver who drove me to the Hastings House when I first arrived on Salt Spring; he is once again my gentle, rescuing giant. He has brought along his friend Jasmine who offers to drive my car to Kayla's house while Oak takes me.

Oak bundles me in a blanket in the passenger seat and presses a thermos of hot tea into my trembling hands.

"You sure know how to get yourself into a whole lot of trouble fast," he says with a low chuckle, "Salt Spring sometimes does that to people, especially if you're hanging out with Kayla."

CHAPTER 6

THE MIDDLE WAY

I am frozen to the bone and still shaking, despite a blazing fire in the stone hearth and a belly full of comfort food — chicken stew with chunky potatoes and carrots. Kayla sits at the far end of the sofa, watching me over the rim of her teacup, patient, letting me set the pace of our conversation.

My eyes flit around the spacious, spartanly furnished living room: twin, olive gray couches, a maple coffee table, chrome lamps, built-in bookshelves and a few large pieces of black-and-white photo art of nude bodies suffused in light and shadow. Panels of glass fill the north and south walls, one side framing the twinkling lights of the distant Vancouver skyline and the other offering the blank, black face of the uninterrupted dark of Kayla's five-acre, forested property.

A framed photo on the mantelpiece catches my attention: Kayla with a handsome, dark-haired man and an equally handsome teenager, who I guess to be her husband David and her son Josh. A small pile of presents, stacked neatly under a wreath of cedar branches and holly berries, reminds me that tomorrow is Christmas Eve.

"Where is your family?" I ask.

"David and Josh are in Vancouver with David's parents," Kayla says, "They always leave me to my own devices for the

Winter Solstice, and Josh loves the time with his grandparents. They'll be back early tomorrow afternoon."

Unexpectedly, big, fat tears well up and spill down my cheeks.

"Sarah, what's going on?" Kayla says.

I turn away and stare sightlessly out the black windows. My whole body is rigid and trembling, with my breath trapped in my upper torso and my stomach cramped, like I'm trying to push something down in me and keep it from the revealing light and the prying eyes of others. But what I'm pushing down pushes back up just as fiercely: my hunger, my awe, my grief, my fear and other things, secret and brewing, that I can sense but not grasp. My mouth fights against the clenched pressure of my jaw; it opens and then shuts, and then opens again, pushing out dry, sobbing puffs of air.

A gentle touch pries my empty teacup from my fingers. Kayla kneels in front of me and takes my cold hands in her warm ones.

"Talk to me," she says, "Maybe I can help."

There is no judgment in her voice, nothing that indicates she thinks less of me after rescuing me from my own stupidity on Mount Maxwell. Nor any of the predatory undertones I'm used to in my working life where exposure of a flaw or signs of vulnerability can cost you your reputation, if not your job. I force myself to look at Kayla. Her face tilts upward toward mine and is filled with tender concern. For a long moment, we gaze into each others' eyes. I soften, begin to breathe more freely and then open my heart and let Kayla in.

"The Dark Goddess, all this magic," I say, working my mouth into a grimace, "it's not just a story, make believe, it's real isn't it?"

"Yes it's real," Kayla says, "You don't need to believe in the

Goddess, you just need to experience Her. Then you know, in your body and your soul, that She is real and can change your life."

My gut muscles seize up and I force myself to ask, "And the story of Inanna and Ereshkigal — is that real as well? Do you have to lose everything, like Inanna, to follow the Dark Goddess's path?"

The logs in the fireplace collapse in on each other, sending up a cascade of sparks before settling into gentle flames and slow-burning embers. Outside the wind battles with the trees, rushing through their needled foliage and knocking their heavy limbs up against each other.

Kayla shifts to sit beside me. As she lets go of my hands, they reflexively ball into fists.

"Tell me what has happened since the ritual," she says.

"My Opa, he has leukemia — he's going to die, leave me, I'll be alone," I say with the words tangling in my throat and competing with my tears, "And my job, my career — two of my co-workers are trying to sabotage me — all since the ritual."

"Oh, Sarah, I'm really sorry about your grandfather and your job," Kayla says, her gaze not wavering from mine, "And you think these things have happened because of the promise you made to Ereshkigal?"

I nod and then blurt out, "It's my fault that Opa Kass is sick! I saw him dead at my feet during the ritual. I saw what Ereshkigal did to Inanna. Still I said yes to Her when She asked me to follow the Dark Goddess's path. And — God help me — even if I could do it over, I'm sure I'd say yes again."

Kayla touches the middle of my brow and says, "Do you remember Ereshkigal's words when you said yes to Her?"

"So it is chosen, so it will be," I say, and then sense the tingling outline of a star under Kayla's fingertips.

"Those words are a vow that hold the Dark Goddess's promise to guide and support your journey," Kayla says, "You started this journey even before the ritual, on the night the raven visited you in Toronto and you said yes to your soul and your hunger. Yes is a very potent magical word; it tells the powers of life that you are ready to show up to your soul work. When you say yes, change happens."

I sense Ereshkigal's shimmering power superimposed over Kayla's physical form, speaking to me through Kayla's words. My heart, my core and my soul respond — aching, ravenous — reaching for the Dark Goddess as I feel Her reaching for me. A yes arises within me, overriding my reason and my resistance, compelling me, Pied-Piper-like, to follow once more where She leads. But no — stop — stop! I can't go there! I can't! I scrunch into a small ball, locking myself down, choking the life out of myself, my agony etched in the rigid lines that mark the constricted muscles of my mouth, jaw and throat.

"But why does She ask so much of me, Kayla — my Opa Kass, my job?" I say, squeezing out the words.

Kayla doesn't respond immediately. A bone-deep cold seems to seep in from the dark windowpanes and she adds another log to the ebbing fire. Her calico cat, Shire, purrs contentedly on the warm hearthstones. Then Kayla reaches for the teapot and refills both of our cups.

"Here, sit up," she says, lightly rubbing my mid-back.

I force myself into an upright position and wrap my hands around the cup. Steamy wisps of lemon and mint caress my jittery senses. I take a sip and a sweet touch of honey soothes my throat and insides. The wind and trees have made their peace and nothing disturbs our silence, save Shire's low, serene rumblings.

"I can't answer your question," Kayla says after we finish

our tea, "I don't know what has made your grandfather sick or whether you will lose your job. But I can tell you that whatever is happening isn't some price or punishment exacted by the Dark Goddess, nor is it random. Your life is your teacher and whatever comes to you is the work of your soul. Things are never as they appear on the surface. Your lessons are woven into your losses and challenges, and only you can figure out what they mean and allow them to change you."

A deep-belly sigh eases my constricted muscles and I straighten my slouched posture. I'm not causing these bad things, at least not directly. And the Dark Goddess isn't demanding a blood price to follow Her path.

"Beauty born of our wounding; things having to die before something new can be born," I say quietly to myself, remembering Will's insights about his divorce.

"Exactly," Kayla says, a ghost of a smile brushing her lips, "That's the heart of Dark Goddess magic. Our beauty and wounding are mirrors of each other. And it's usually our pain and struggles that help us understand what we need to heal and change in our lives. But positive things have happened as well haven't they? You were beautiful at the Winter Solstice ritual and showed the true courage of a person of power; it was your kiss that brought Inanna back to life."

I wish Kayla wouldn't look at me that way, seeing beauty and power that aren't there, just like Will.

She passes me a box of kleenex and I blow my nose and wipe my eyes. There must be big blotches of mascara running down my cheeks, but when I glance at the tissue I don't detect any telltale, black smears. Oh right, I skipped the makeup routine this morning, and brushing my hair and my teeth for that matter. My jeans are ripped and I haven't showered for almost two days. Where is my beauty now?

In a quick, birdlike movement, my palms flutter to my solar plexus; that's where my true beauty resides, inside of me, waiting for me to show up and claim her. Yes, powerful things have happened since I came to Salt Spring. I've found what I was looking for: the lost treasure of my feminine soul. But I can't touch her and I'm terrified to take the next step and make her mine. Kayla and Will are mistaken. I'm not powerful or courageous. I look down at my lap, at the floor, at my distorted image reflected back from the mirrored surface of the darkened windows, anywhere but at Kayla.

"You still haven't told me what happened on Mount Maxwell," Kayla says.

What happened on Mount Maxwell — something vast and beyond words — and something that so clearly reveals my smallness of being. Kayla is backing me into a corner and probing a shadowy place that I'd prefer stay hidden.

"It's hard to explain," I say, my voice flat and expressionless, "I was at the cliff's edge, sketching the valley, and a raven leapt into the air in front of me. I became a raven, flying beside her. Not in my body, I don't think, but in my imagination. But it felt so real, like a more solid, physical version of a dream. Then the raven was gone and I was back in my human body. That's when I got lost and called you."

"Wow, that's remarkable, Sarah!" Kayla says, "How can you be so nonchalant? What you're describing is shape-shifting; you entered the raven's reality and took on her form. No wonder you were disoriented and couldn't find the path again. Big magic will do that to you."

My head snaps back to face Kayla. I feel my cheeks flare and then blanch.

"Maybe it was remarkable," I say, "But it was also cruel, giving me that big a taste of magic and then shoving me back into my little mind. I don't know how to do this stuff. I've been flung into these wild experiences and then flung back out again. And all I've accomplished is messing up the things I care about most, my Opa and my job. God, I think I'm losing my sanity. Can't I just go back to Toronto and forget any of this ever happened?"

For the first time since we've met, Kayla seems to lose her composure. She looks away from me and rubs the heel of her hand across her furrowed brow. Her face clouds over as if she is reliving a bad memory.

When Kayla turns to me and speaks, her tone is subdued and pained, "Yes you can go home and leave these experiences behind. But once you wake up, even a little, you can never really go back to sleep. The longings of our soul are powerful things. When we get a taste of our true beauty and of magic, we only hunger for them more."

I squirm on the couch, itchy and restless within my own skin. I don't know whether I should get up and leave or beg Kayla to help me sort out these confusing, compelling mysteries. I don't want to stay and I don't want to go. That Mount Maxwell cliff looms before me with the raven seducing me to leap and fly. But if I leap, I'm afraid my life is going to fall apart. And I'll end up like Great Aunt Beatrice — shriveled up and mad — out of the game and out of control.

"I've failed you," Kayla continues, resting her hand upon my arm, "I knew you had a huge experience at the Winter Solstice ritual and I should have arranged to meet with you before now. I know what it's like to be flung into big magic unprepared and unsupported. You never should have gone to Mount Maxwell by yourself. You needed a friend, Sarah, someone to help you with your deep work. I'm so sorry I've let you down."

I glower at Kayla, wanting to dislike and distrust her so I can turn my back on her and on the Dark Goddess. But what I see are the faint glimmer of light around her edges, the loose and easy way she holds her body, and the kindness and compassion in her eyes. And I want, desperately, what she has. Kayla has not failed me. I have failed myself. She was there for me, but I pushed her, and that piece of the Dark Goddess simmering in her blue irises, away.

My shoulders sag as my impulse to fight leaves me. A profound sadness, tinged with an infinite sense of loss and lostness, hovers just below the surface of my flight instincts. Not only because of Opa Kass's illness and the threat to my job, but also because this world of magic has made me aware of who I am not, what I do not have in my life, and the gap that exists between my fumbling experiences and Kayla's subtle, expansive power that slips between her words like melted honey — delicious, nourishing and natural. Once again tears come, hot and unbidden, and with them a hot shame that I am not enough, out of my league, but too far down this road to back out.

Kayla gathers me into her arms and rocks me. I don't have words for these things that twist and tangle me up, but the feelings are there as quivering bundles of energy and tremulous body sensations. And I let Kayla inside of me, deeper than I've ever let anyone before. I sense her brushing up against my fears and my desires, my shame and my hopes, my certainty that I cannot, will not, walk away from her and my barely suppressed urge to bolt in the opposite direction.

When my crying slows, Kayla takes my wet face between her strong hands and speaks to the place in me that shimmers between my desires and my fears, "You are enough, Sarah, for me, for the Dark Goddess and for the magic coming into your life. All that matters is what you truly, deeply want. Do you want to turn away from this journey or continue to follow where it leads? That is the only thing you need to decide right now."

I close my eyes and hear the echoes of Opa Kass's wisdom: everything you need is within you; deep inside you know what matters most to you.

My hands move to the center of my body. I sense the soft, even breath of my sleeping beauty, my feminine soul, stretched out on the green earth in her white gown. And I want, more than anything else in the whole world, to kiss her ruby lips awake.

"I'd like to continue," I say, barely above a whisper, "But I don't know what to do."

The fire, burnt down to ash and embers, casts an eerie, red glow around the darkened room. The only illumination comes from a pair of candles on the coffee table and a distant light above the kitchen stove. Flickering shadows shimmy up the walls and play with the contours of Kayla's facial features.

"Maybe we can take the next step together," Kayla says, "I had a dream last night that was a summons from the Dark Goddess, and my instincts tell me that I'm supposed to bring you with me. Would you like to hear about my dream?"

Kayla's sly smile sends a little electric jolt down my spine. My nose begins to quiver and I sense a faint change in the air: a smoky heat emanating from Kayla and a responding heat arising from me. Goosebumps skitter across my skin. I rest my back against the arm of the couch and curl my legs around me.

"Yes," I say, "Yes please."

"In the dream, I walk down a deserted road surrounded by total darkness," Kayla says, leaning in toward me, "I'm wearing a red cloak and dusty boots. Three wild dogs trot alongside me, with matted, black fur and eyes like glowing coals. I know they are dog-men — shape-shifters that can take on human form. A hearth fire appears in the distance. Its flames call to me and I start to run. When I reach the fire circle's perimeter, I stop, knowing that something momentous will happen when I step from the dark into its light. I wake up just as the dogs push me into the fire circle. I believe the Dark Goddess Hecate sent me the dream."

Scarlet embers reflect in Kayla's widened pupils, as if she's still entranced by her hearth-fire dream. Her upper body sways slightly and my body mimics hers; slow, sensuous movements spiral from my shoulders through my torso to my hips, and then back up again.

"Tell me more," I say, "Tell me about Hecate."

"Hecate comes from Greek mythology," Kayla says, "The dream is full of Her symbols: the magical dogs, the number three, the pathway in the dark and the beckoning light. She is the Goddess of magic and the triple crossroads where our destiny is woven by the choices we make. I know Hecate well. She's been with me since the beginning of my spiritual journey."

As Kayla talks, I sense another presence in the room, hazy and indeterminate, as if speaking Hecate's name has caught Her attention, but She hasn't fully joined us. For a brief second, my shoulders tense up and my nose sniffs the air for danger, but then my curiosity gets the better of me.

"What does the dream mean?" I ask.

"Dreams speak in symbols," Kayla says, "I wear a red cloak that marks me as a SheBard: a priestess and person of power in the Goddess tradition. The hearth fire is an ancient meeting place for sharing visions and tales. I think the dream is an invitation; Hecate is calling to us as Her priestesses, and She has stories to share at Her hearth fire. One way to find out for sure is to enter the dream in ritual space and see where it leads."

With a wide, playful grin, she adds, "Are you in?"

Am I in? — a simple question that packs a heavy punch. An equally simple yes will land me at the edge of that hearth-fire circle, primed to step from the dark into its light. And who knows what will happen after that? I've lost my naivety when it comes to magic and ritual. Change will come and most likely not change of my choosing. Am I mad going ahead with this after everything that has happened? Maybe I've cried out my brains along with my doubts, regardless, it's too late to be asking this question; I'm already in.

"Well, I might be in just for the clothes," I say, matching Kayla's grin, "Do I get a fabulous red cloak like yours?"

"There's a good chance," Kayla says, "But of course you have to earn it."

"Fair enough," I say, "Then yes, absolutely, I'm in!"

We sit facing each other, cross-legged on cushions on the floor, in a special room reserved for Kayla's spiritual practice. Four beeswax candles softly illuminate the directional corners of the space, one each in the North, East, South and West. Shire joins us and I hear her quiet rustles as she makes herself comfortable on a nearby cushion.

"Our magic tonight will be more improvised than the Winter Solstice ritual," Kayla says, "We're going to do trance work where we enter the hearth-fire dream together and see where it leads us. It's tricky, but you've had a taste of similar, spontaneous magic when you shape-shifted and flew with the raven on Mount Maxwell. We'll have the benefit of being able to talk to each other and share what we're feeling and seeing. I'll get us started and then we'll go from there. Okay?"

"Okay," I say, though I have no idea how to do any of these things or even what they mean.

With a shake of her shoulders, Kayla closes her eyes and her facial features soften. Once again a smoky heat rises from her skin and light glimmers around her form. She places her palm flat against my solar plexus and I mirror her actions. My fingers feel sticky and damp and I can't control their slight tremor. Her touch fills me with a strange melange of sensations, some tender and soothing, others fierce and wild, tugging me into the swirling currents of her dream world. I feel my heart flitting about inside my ribs, like a startled bird in a cage.

"Close your eyes and loosen your jaw and your backbone," Kayla says, her voice melodic and pitched slightly lower than usual, "Sense the solid ground beneath you, holding and supporting your body. Focus on the effortless sensations of breath. Feel the rising and falling of your chest — the cool rush of air in through your nose — the warm release out through your nose. Breath brings quiet, calm, emptiness. Breath synchronizes our energy in accordance with the ancient laws of life — steady, constant, never ending. Breath opens the gateways to the mysteries that await us, below the below of the world that we know."

As Kayla speaks, my body begins to relax; my shoulders drop and my knees sink closer to the floor. I absorb the steady in and out movement of Kayla's chest and belly through my flat palm, and my heart begins to mimic the even, comforting cadence of her heartbeat. Soon our breath is synchronized and I center my attention on its slow, full rise and fall.

"Gently remove your awareness from your outer knowing and focus it inward," Kayla says, "Imagine you've turned off the lights in your house and you're carrying a single candle to find your way in the dark. Quiet the voices and noises of the everyday world: the creaking of the wind in the trees, the ticking clock, and the constant ramblings inside your head. Still your waking mind's fears and expectations; traveling between the worlds is not its game. Pay attention instead to the sensations and sounds of your inner landscape: the near-silent flow of breath-in, breath-out, the slight beat and pulse of heart and blood, and the tug of gravity on bones."

At first my gut tightens and my mind resists Kayla's suggestions, holding on, like gripped fingers, to my everyday sensibilities. But no, I'm not going to hold back, not now. I turn my focus back to my breath, and, like a flower closing its petals at sundown, I gather my senses inward, shutting out the tinkling wind chimes outside the window, Shire's delicate snores, and the hard, grumbling voices in my mind. A tingling sensation spirals up my spine, over the back of my skull and down the front of my body. My perception widens and deepens; I open to the caress of silver moonlight on my skin, the pauses between one breath and the next, and the pregnant emptiness within me.

"Allow your body to become spacious and light," Kayla continues, "more like backlit clouds than firm, fleshy clay, shifting your awareness away from your physical form and into the unbounded, wild powers of your dreambody. Step with me, dreambody to dreambody, over a border that separates the narrow vision of the waking world from the limitless sea of the dream realm. Imagine passing through the gentle, brushing touch of a wall of shimmering mist that winnows out the laws and ways of the physical Universe. As we come out the other side, we fully enter the dreaming where we can go anywhere and be anything, like in our nighttime sleep adventures."

Our hands slip into the space between us, with Kayla's fingers loosely intertwined with mine and our breath unified

— slow, slow in — slow, slow out. I have no sense of where her flesh ends and mine begins, nor whether we are still woven of muscle and bone. The electric pulse of her essence streams through me as her dream knowing infuses mine. And I transit from physical to dreaming reality, trading a limiting consciousness for a delicious otherness, as enticing and free as a springtime breeze.

"Sarah, feel the dreaming drink in our presence," Kayla says, "And our most sacred hungers and desires. Imagine that we are stepping together into the inky darkness of my dream. Beneath our feet is a dirt road, hard-packed and unyielding, that will lead us to the waiting hearth fire. When I look down at myself, I am wearing my red cloak, wrapped tight around me for warmth, and tawny deerskin boots caked with red dust. Tell me what you see."

I open my dream eyes onto a murky, formless world.

"I don't see much of anything," I say, "But I sense doors, endless doors, around me in every direction."

"Track my voice," Kayla says, "and let it lead you to the door of my hearth-fire dream."

Decisively I turn to my left, walk a few paces and then stretch out my hands.

"I've found the door," I say, "I can sense you. You are right in front of me, standing on the dirt road and reaching for me. But I can't touch you. And I can't see you. Kayla, where are you? Where are you?"

There is no answer. And then I lose even my tentative sense that Kayla is somewhere nearby. I can't feel her presence or hear her voice. I am alone and lost within this infinite, enveloping darkness, with only the jagged rasps of my breath for company.

My temples begin to map out a painful beat, and my belly lurches and refluxes an acidic backwash that coats my tongue and curdles my resolve to continue this dreamwork ritual. I scent the air around me and cower at the unfamiliar, fusty, underbelly odors of a place that has never felt the kiss of sunshine.

"Kayla, Kayla!" I shout into the darkness, but only the muted, muffled echo of my desperate voice comes back to me.

A cold, hard stone lodges in my stomach and freezes my brain and limbs into a single line of thought: I need to get out of here! Forget Kayla! Forget this crazy dream quest! Just get me out of here now!

No, no, not yet. I take several deep breaths. I won't let this beat me. I want to be here and work this through. What do you want from me, Hecate? I've followed where I've been led, said yes every step of the way. I've been stripped bare, but still I am here. So what do you want from me now, Hecate? What?

Absolute silence. Hecate cannot answer my questions. I need to figure this one out on my own.

I focus my attention inward, willing myself to be calm, and imagine my dream eyes breaking through the dense shadows that block my vision, woven, I suspect, of my fears. The dreaming responds. My perception shifts and I find myself in a misted, insubstantial world, hued in silvered tones of charcoal gray and deep purple; a twilight realm held in stasis between day and night, and the ending of one road and the beginning of the next.

When I look down at myself, I'm dressed in the same outfit I wore to Kayla's house, with my jeans still ripped at the knee. But my body appears wispy and insubstantial, like the surrounding landscape, as if I too am stuck mid-metamorphosis, caught between one choice and the next.

With a few more slow, calm breaths, my vision further widens. A jolt of relief fires up my guts and then rises up my spine and pops the tension building in my skull cap. I'm wrong about Kayla. She is here, to one side of me, though I can only make out the vague outline of red that must be her SheBard cloak. Something in this twilight dreamscape stops me from seeing her more clearly and from joining her on that hard-packed road that leads to Hecate's hearth fire.

A voice growls right behind me, "Think again, girl-woman. Nothing wrong with the dreaming. Must be you."

I know immediately who has joined me by the feral musk of wild dog; it's not so much an odor of unwashed fur and body, as a sensual, pheromonal blend that invokes days spent amongst green-growing things and nights under the starry sky. He is one of Hecate's dog-men in his human form, though his canine nature beams through his thick, matted, soot-colored hair and his muscular, long-limbed physique.

He sniffs me and I sniff him in return, each prowling around the other in a low, creature-like crouch. Our nostrils twitch and flare, taking in quick, small sips of each others' essence.

With a toothy grin, he barks a laugh at me and says, "Maybe not so tame and useless."

We stare at each other, keeping our distance, and I'm not afraid. A part of me knows him; I've met him before or someone like him. I recognize the raw, unadorned power of his body, the spark of bristling alertness in his eyes and his regal, wide-legged stance that mark his surety of purpose and place in this dream realm. And he is a truth speaker. The dreaming isn't the problem — I am. And until I figure out why, he's not going to let me onto Hecate's path.

"You're like Neti, the gatekeeper of Ereshkigal's realm," I say, looking straight into his dark, smoldering eyes, "but you guard Hecate's path."

"Girl-woman has eyes that see, but not true power," he

snarls, "Boy-man power is strong. Woman-witch power is weak. But belly is hungry, hungry for the Mother."

The dog-man points to the right of where we stand, extending a single, bronze-skinned finger with a curved, claw-like nail. The mutable mist of this place solidifies into a paved-over, asphalt road, bordered by grimy snowbanks. In the far distance, I glimpse a gray cityscape, with skyscrapers frosted over by the harsh brush of winter. Then he points to the left and another road materializes, this one of dark brown earth, hemmed in on either side by lush foliage of waxen, chartreuse leaves and exuberant, fleshy splashes of orange, red and purple flowers. The road itself indicates some form of human presence, yet the feral tendrils of the green-growing realm overleap any attempts at taming its unruly nature. The roadways intersect at our feet and extend diagonally as far as the eye can see in front and behind us.

Kayla's earlier lesson on Hecate comes back to me.

"Hecate's crossroads of choice," I say, "Where our choices determine our destiny."

"Two roads, two ways of power, two ways of dreaming," the dog-man says, "Time to choose, girl-woman."

With trepidation, I step onto the paved-over path; it's the more familiar of the two and, oddly enough, more comforting — the demon you know. The winter landscape vanishes and I'm standing at the border of the familiar, well-manicured grounds of the private middle school I attended in my youth. There's an autumn chill and a fermentation of leaves in the air. My heart rate accelerates as a long-repressed memory, an etched moment frozen in time, begins to thaw before my dream eyes.

My younger self sprints to the far end of the grounds, my legs pumping madly and my breath coming in aching gasps, with a pack of rabid girls close on my heels — girls that I had vainly hoped would be my friends. I wear a jade green coat — part of my Grade 7 back-to-school ensemble — its fur collar and cuffs still white and spotless. My parents transferred me to this prestigious institution in my second year of middle school, making me the new kid on the block.

An eight-foot, chain-link fence blocks my path, but it's my only route to safety so I scrabble up one side and down the other, scoring the unblemished skin of my black leather boots. I jump the last couple of feet, crumbling to the ground, but quickly pick myself up and turn to my enemies, panting and soaked in fear sweat. The girls snarl and hiss, hurling insults like mud that smears goo on my tender insides. My brand-new coat has collected its own dirt and oily smudges, and I add to the muck by absently rubbing my clammy palms up and down its soft, velvet nap. The movement soothes me and helps me block out their stabbing words. But I can't block out the naked hatred and scorn that distend their flushed, young faces.

I'm one of the brainy kids in class, the teacher's-pet type, aching to have the right answer and outshine my fellow students. And I am pretty: a girl beginning to morph into womanhood with promising, early signs of the curves to come, big, blue eyes and a stellar wardrobe. In the stratified dynamics of schoolyard politics, I'm an anomaly, a freak, in need of testing and categorization.

At dinner that night, I poke at my chicken cacciatore and avert my gaze as my mother scolds me about my soiled coat and damaged boots. But I don't leak a word about what happened to me and excuse myself from the table with my food untouched. Nor do I rush into the principal's office to lodge a complaint the next day, though my stomach feels twisted in knots and my face takes on the pallor of the dead when the recess bell rings.

Outside, I keep my back to the brown brick wall and stay close to the double-glass doors of the side entrance.

The girl mob finds me quick enough, forms a semi-circle around me to block my escape options, and then coldly stares me up and down in a game of psychological chicken. I stay still but keep eye contact, and, most importantly, I counter my attackers with the corner of my mouth curled in a defiant, silent snarl. Minutes pass, no more than ten or fifteen because recess hasn't ended yet, and then, by an invisible signal, they collectively feign disinterest and strut off en masse, leaving me alone in my victory.

Later that afternoon and over the next few days, these girls, individually and in clumps of two or three, start to interact with me, civilly at first, and then with increasing warmth and enthusiasm. The tension in my jaw softens to a smile with every encounter, and my contracted breath widens into a puffed-out chest of pride. I've survived the initiation and within the week the mob girls are my best friends, granting me the full membership rights of "The Group" — the eight powerful, popular girls who are the true rulers of this place.

I have no idea how I warranted this change in status from freak to cool, from unworthy to worthy, and from hunted to a member of the royal pack. For an extended moment, the memory vision plays on and I watch my younger self assimilate The Group's power ethos: mimicking the other girls' attitudes and judgments, playing by their cruel rules of who is in and who is out, and conforming to their standards of dress, even down to the minutia of hairclips and lipstick shade. The cocky sway of my hips and exaggerated swish of my hair speak volumes of my sense of privilege and status as a member of the much envied and lauded in-crowd.

What happened to those mob girls? I dig around in the dusty

recesses of my mind, but I can't recall seeing or speaking to any of them when we went our separate ways after middle school. They vanished from my world even though they were the center of my post-pubescent universe. But the primal lesson they carved into the reptilian, survival part of my brain has certainly remained — life comes with two options: the misery plan for the outcast and the happy plan for the beautiful. In one you run like a dog from a murdering throng, and in the other you strut like a queen, basking in privilege and power.

The middle school scene fades and dissolves into eddies of mist that rearrange themselves into a much more recent memory; this one is from the early daylight hours of last Friday as I dress myself for a very special work event: the announcement of my promotion to partner. From the wide-angle perspective of the dreaming, I witness my adult self in this variation of my habitual morning routine.

I stand between the opposing walls of my walk-in closet, one side lined with business wear and the other with my supplementary wardrobe categories: casual, evening, yoga and visits with my mother. I'm selecting from my extensive collection of gray, black and navy suits, white and cream tailored shirts, black and navy pumps and matching purses — all monotone, subdued, sexless and very expensive. I don't even glance at the other wall, with its splashes of scarlet red and midnight blue and full display of my boot fetish. There is no way in hell I'd let out even a peep of this other me at the office — the one who emerges from this closet on weekends wrapped in delicious, feminine folds of sensuous fabric and bold color, and the thigh-high sex appeal of stiletto-heeled boots.

Decisively, I reach for my most expensive black suit and most modest white shirt, consciously calculating the best look to fend off possible attack from my sharp-eyed, sharp-tongued co-workers, and the inevitable backlash of my elevation to partner status. Marsha, Trent and many of my senior, male colleagues are potential enemies that I need to protect myself from.

With the deeper vision of my dream knowing, I detect the warrior-like squaring of my shoulders and tensing of my muscles as I don my dark-suited armor and fortify myself for battle in a man's world. My makeup is precisely applied in muted, natural shades that subtly highlight my blue eyes and ample lips — just a touch of femininity, as per my mother's training. For this special day, I leave off my signature perfume; I don't need to call extra attention to the fact that I smell different, and nicer, than the men I'll be having lunch with.

Every workday morning, I do a version of this routine and then spend the rest of the day in a state of constant vigilance, knowing that I have to act like a man, actually a better man than all the rest, while somehow still displaying subtle indications of my womanhood. Unspoken rules dominate my actions, derived from a fine balance between beauty and brains, the secret boys' club ethos, and the even more secret, girl-against-girl rivalry. This is the price of my power and success and of retaining my privileged membership in the upper ranks of the corporate world.

As I watch this clear reflection of my grownup, everyday self, I slide down the closet wall and rest my elbows on my knees. A tear traces an icy track on the right side of my face. I want so badly to shake her, me, awake. Despite my hard work and achievements, I'm constantly dancing to tunes outside of myself. My boss, my work colleagues, my mother, the world at large, even my dead father, all of them have more say on how I live my life than I do myself. Day in, day out, I push to be the best, to please, to conform, to outperform and to make sure I'm a winner. Damn, I'm still that bullied adolescent girl chasing the happy-plan option. Safe — I want to be safe and liked — and then no one can hurt me or push me around. My whole body goes rigid. No, oh my God, no! This is a lie, a ruse! Nothing can guarantee my safety — not a Harvard MBA and partner position, nor good looks, grooming or manners. Marsha and Trent — that's what they're up to with their spreading of rumors and rigging the reorganization — they are schoolyard bullies using dirty tricks to bring me down. There's no safe place, not even at the top of the pile. Not for me, Matt, Marsha or Trent because there's always a bigger, more ruthless bully. And even he or she doesn't ultimately set the rules.

This last thought clears my mind and calms me. The paved-over road sets these frigid, sterile rules: obey, conform, outshine and grab what you can before someone else does because power, money, food, even love are limited resources, doled out in limited proportions to the limited ranks of the deserving. This is the dominant message that drives a person seeking power on the paved-over road, with its power-over ethos defined and imposed from the outside in. And it's these rules that have driven me as a girl surviving the test of middle school social mores, as a woman bent on succeeding in a man's world, and as a human being trying to make the best of my life and my talents. Fear is the unholy stench of this road that strangles me now and strangles me every day of my life, trapping me in a game that is toxic and destructive to both the winners and the losers. But it is not the only way of power, nor the only choice of how to live and dream my life. There is another road, another way.

Like a pinpricked balloon, this vision deflates in on itself, leaving me pale and trembling in the winter-deadened land-scape of the paved-over road. My nose twitches with the toxic vapors of its asphalt surface and the lingering stench of my adolescent self ordeal those many years ago.

Resolutely, I withdraw myself from this landscape and return to the intersecting space between the two roads. The dog-man rests on his haunches, his body relaxed and his attention never leaving me. He is still and silent, seemingly unaffected by my experiences, but I suspect he has entered and witnessed my dream visions as clearly as I have.

As I move onto the green-growing road, the luscious foliage and earthen path immediately disappear and reform into another memory vision from my childhood. This time I peek from the far corner of Opa Kass's livingroom into a precious remembrance from about six years of age, or so I would guess from my straight-bang haircut and the girlhood roundness of my cheeks.

We curl up beside each other on his scruff-marked, brown leather sofa, with books in front of our noses and empty cocoa mugs close at hand. My stomach rumbles loudly and we both laugh. Then Opa starts our favorite game: heart's desire.

"What do you want for lunch, my sweet Sarah?" he asks.

His hands over my eyes cue me that this is no ordinary question; I must look deep, deep inside for the answer, and if I truly name my heart's desire, he will do his best to help my wish come true.

"Hmmm," I say, scrunching my eyelids closed and cupping my palms against my stomach, "Belly, belly, what do you need today?"

After a lengthy pause, I say, "Sausages, Opa — those yummy ones from the Italian butcher — and that hot, spicy mustard — oh, and those sweet and sour pickles from the deli on the next block."

He gives me a noisy, lip-smacking kiss on my forehead and

then says, "Let's bundle up and go. Sausages, mustard and pickles it is!"

More of these same memories flash by.

"What shall we draw, my Sarah?" Opa asks.

"Pretty world, pretty world, what do you want to share with us today?" I say, stretching out my beauty-divining fingertips and following where they lead. Then we stop, my sensitive digits quivering, in front of Opa's apple trees and their white-petal clouds of freshly opened blossoms. On another day, a gang of copper-backed beetles, digging in the compost pile, calls to me, and even once, Opa Kass's brand-new, black Mercedes, glistening with water drops from its morning carwash.

"What do you want for your birthday, Opa?" I ask, and my little hands over his wrinkled eyes remind him that he has to answer true and fair.

"Just one more day with your Oma," he answers with a quiver in his voice that tells me he still misses her, though she died a long time ago, "so she would get to meet you and love you like I do."

My grownup heart aches at the longing in my Opa's voice and with my bittersweet knowing that, all too soon, he will be granted his wish of reuniting with my Oma Hannah. I want nothing more than to enfold him in my arms and cry with him. But this is a dream vision of the past, and I can only watch my child self act in my stead, awkwardly patting Opa's knee and offering him a crumbling morsel of peanut butter cookie.

When did I stop believing in this game of heart's desire? Probably around the same time I gave up art, nature and my weekly Sundays with Opa Kass. Or maybe earlier still, writing it off as mere childhood fantasy. Or has it been dormant within me, waiting for someone special to reawaken it? My fingers tug at the blue bead necklace, my treasure gift from Emilie, hanging next to my skin and close to my heart. Didn't Emilie inspire me to go on a treasure hunt in search of my lost jewels? No one put hands over my eyes, but wasn't I searching, true and fair, for my soul's desire? And didn't that little treasure hunt game lead me directly to Kayla and Selena, the Winter Solstice ritual and my vision of my Goddess self? Everything I need to know, what matters most to me, is within me. Opa's heart's-desire magic hasn't left me. He is still helping my wishes come true.

The childhood scene with Opa Kass dissipates and tumbles to the ground, like shining motes of dust. A new memory arises, this one from my ritual vision on Winter Solstice eve. But it is different than the other dream memories because I'm no longer watching the action from the outside. I'm inside the memory itself, picking up the scene from where I'd left off.

I stare into the obsidian mirror of black, polished rock. The surface becomes transparent and my lost Goddess self stands in front of me. As before, she is dressed in a simple, white gown, with snake bracelets on her arms and a silver circlet upon her brow. This time I savor the connection and really take her in. She is the spitting image of me with large, blue eyes framed by long lashes, shoulder-length, honey blonde hair, an athletic build, contrasted by a teasing hint of full breasts and hips, and the same beauty mark under the left cheekbone. But she stands taller and prouder than I do, exuding a queenly nature that I lack.

Unlike our first encounter, her body appears translucent and I can see the play of energy that underlies her outer form. A white-hot ember, sparkling and pulsing like the beating heart of a star, hangs suspended in the space above her solar plexus. Ripples of power radiate upward and downward from this ember, in shimmering waves of heat and light.

My hands press into my mid-body and I feel this star

ember in my own core. A presence, infinitely holy, reaches out to me through the layers of my flesh, bypassing a lifetime of disconnection, to bond me with my secret essence. Pulses of electric current course through my body, subtly adjusting my configuration of bone and tissue to more perfectly align my outside with my inside: a slight extension of the lift of my head and its balance on my spine, the melding of the shape of my soles to the contours of the land, and a richer cadence of heartbeat and tremor of nerve impulses.

I sense Opa Kass's hands over my eyes and his voice close by my ear, "What do you want, sweet Sarah? What does your heart truly desire?"

I am that pause between one breath and the next, with the endless doors of the dream world spread out before me. And whatever choice I make at this moment will most certainly determine my destiny.

With eyes closed, one hand on my heart and the other on my belly, I look deep, deep inside. I see a touch of strawberry-tinted whipped cream at the corner of Emilie's mouth, and her wise, clear gaze as she shares her secret knowledge that Salt Spring is a treasure island. I smell Will's bergamot-scented skin and taste his pulsing throat under my hot mouth as the earth and stars make love through our fully clothed bodies. I hear Ereshkigal's wild wails rising up from the rock and forest of the Fulford Valley and feel Her coursing through my fingers as I slash Her death-red grief and mine onto my sketchbook page. And I see the reflection of scarlet embers in Kayla's eyes, feel her strong hands cradling my wet cheeks, and I know, really truly know, that I am enough. Inanna's cold lips brought back to life by my kiss — my shape-shifting flight with the raven into the reality beyond the concrete wall — I want to be alive, fully, radically, deliciously alive. This is my true heart's desire.

I can't turn away from this moment — it's time to say yes, to surrender, to trust — no matter the cost.

I step through the obsidian mirror, my way no longer blocked as it was on the Winter Solstice, and come face-to-face with my beautiful Goddess self, her priestess powers intact and awaiting my reclaiming embrace. She holds a blackened iron pot filled with earth and water — the dirt of life from our Solstice ritual.

With a slow, sensuous caress, she paints a mud-smeared star on my brow and says, "Nothing is lost that cannot be refound. I am your soul's desire, your lost treasure, returned to you. If you choose it so, so it will be."

I cup her lovely, ethereal face between my warm hands and kiss her ruby-red lips — slow, sweet and certain.

"Yes," I whisper into her ear.

She vanishes into wisps of silver smoke that slip between the spaces of my physical form, sending shivers of delight across the length of my body. I stand alone, and yet not alone; what was lost from me has been refound and reclaimed, by my own free will and choice, and now rests, a burning ember of starlight, in my inner core.

A freshening breeze blows this vision away, filling my lungs with floral, oxygen-rich air, and I find myself standing on the green-growing road. With each inhalation, I take in a fragment of the untamed fecundity of this place, and on each exhalation, I share a bit of my raw, undomesticated essence. My bones and joints begin to loosen and my hips to rock and sway as we groove, life force to life force, the green world and me.

Yes, oh, yes, yes — this is another way of power, a power-within ethos where my wild, true beauty communes with the wild, true beauty of others. Here there is enough — enough joy, enough nourishment, enough love, enough magic, enough power, enough beauty — for everyone and everything. The green-growing road will always grant us our deepest longings and needs if we live and dream, true and fair, from the inside out. Opa Kass has been trying to teach me these things my whole life.

With a nudge to the small of my back, my dog-man companion pushes me back into the crossroads space between the two divergent roads.

He places the muscled heel of one hand hard against my upper chest and his other against my lower back, and growls into my ear, "Big dreams, girl-woman. Fear power or true-self power? Time to choose, Sarah-woman."

Energy flows from the dog-man into my body, gathering momentum in my core like a brewing storm. With my feet firmly planted and my toes digging into the earth, I close my eyes and turn my awareness inward. Around and around the energy storm spins, sucking chunks of debris into its vortex: broken bits of my memory visions, entangled with silver threads of living light; flashes of fear, hunger, hate, pain, love, joy and wonder, primal emotions unearthed from their dream visions. My hips and torso begin to move in large, counter-clockwise circles as if unraveling me from my insides outward. Loud, forceful breaths push this maelstrom out through my flared nostrils until howling winds whip around my body, tearing away my clothes and battering my exposed flesh.

My flat palms reach out toward the paved-over and the green-growing roads and magnetically draw these opposing, crackling forces into my perfect storm. I stand, stretched taut, in the midst of this chaos, shaking, raw, naked and more joyfully awake than I ever could have imagined.

I throw back my head, my eyes shining wide, and shout, "Yes!"

Yes — I have kissed my Goddess self awake. Yes — I have chosen the green-growing road and its inside-out power. I feel the truth of these things in my very bones and in the singing life in my flesh. I am changed, forever. There is no going back.

Yet the paved-over road is still part of me. Its fear may rule me, but I also sense the strong, vibrant threads of my worldly power, woven of my sweat and talent, and my satisfaction and joy in what I do. I will not abandon my existing life. Nor will I give up this new world of magic.

My body remembers the raven's teachings from our flight together on Mount Maxwell, and I imagine my outstretched arms as wings, riding these wild winds and wild, rival powers with ease and grace. I pull my winged arms inward, gathering these clashing energies in their embracing circle, and then I press them into my solar plexus with my human palms. I open myself up, deep and wide, honoring and ingesting all that I am. The storm slows, calms and dissipates.

I have my answer for the dog-man.

When I look down, I'm now dressed in a white silk gown, an off-white wool coat and butter-soft deerskin boots. My wrists are adorned with silver snake bracelets and a silver circlet crowns my brow.

I turn toward the dog-man and say, "I walk the paved-over and the green-growing roads. Their fear power and true-self power are both part of me. My way forward must honor these truths, so I choose the path between these roads, if such a thing exists."

The dog-man paces around me, taking in several long, slow sniffs of my scent, and then breaks into a broad, fanged smile.

"Ah, girl-woman has soul that knows," he says, "Must be big. Big like world. Big like the Mother. Holy dances with horror — desire with fear — death with life."

He spreads his arms wide and a third road appears, cutting between the other two.

"See, Sarah-woman, the middle road — path of life and true power — the way of the Dark Mother."

Spinning on his heels, the dog-man and the triple crossroads disappear. And there is only one path under my feet, hard-packed and extending into the pitch black landscape.

Kayla stands on this path, with three soot-colored, shaggy dogs gathered around her, red-cloaked and beaming her welcome at me.

CHAPTER 7

PATH OF SHE

Though I am still in the dream world, there is nothing misty or insubstantial about this place. Above us gnarled, shadowy boughs creak and moan in an erratic wind and frame a moonless, starless night sky. I lift one foot and then the other, feeling the magnetic pull of the ground anchoring me in my body and to the land.

The largest of the three dogs, with a star-shaped patch of white fur on his forehead, pushes his bristled snout into my lower back. I close my eyes, nodding my head slightly, as I feel the intense, electric pulse of his presence flow into me. He is the guardian of Hecate's path, my dog-man companion, shifted into his canine shape.

I place my palm on Kayla's chest and feel her heart quicken as the dog-man's energy passes from my flesh into hers. And in this communion, I sense Kayla absorbing everything that transpired between the dog-man and me at Hecate's crossroads.

"You have chosen Hecate's path," she says.

"Yes," I reply, not only to Kayla but to the listening ears of the dream world.

A tremor passes through the soles of my feet and the red earth morphs into a path hewn of red granite paving stones, flecked with tiny glimmers of silver light. The wind shifts and

I take in the smoky resin of a wood fire and the fusty musk of the earth's underbelly. A ball of hot, sparking energy gathers in my solar plexus, and then I sense a distinct, magnetic tug that irresistibly draws me forward.

I feel the same quivering urgency in Kayla as we set off together, her hand squeezed tightly in mine. The dogs run ahead, their hard-muscled bodies brushing past our legs. Though the darkness soon swallows them up, they leave a shimmering, phosphorescent trail in their wake and the air resounds with their sharp barks in the near distance.

Power throbs all around us, as if we are inside a living beast with its life force and pulsing tissues pressing in on us. And we are not alone; unseen beings witness and track our progress. Their hushed murmurs ripple through the profound quiet of this place, and I sense them take my measure in the effervescent stroke of hands of mist against my exposed skin. My hungers and fears cling to me, like the skin-smell of my insides seeping out. I imagine them drawn to this scent, like bees to honey, or like vultures to carrion.

My grip on Kayla's hand tightens as the icy exhalations of our travel companions skitter across the back of my neck. Ghoulish images fill my mind of red-eyed demons peering out from hidden crevasses and the bony fingers of the restless dead grasping at our living light.

"Do you feel them?" I whisper, pulling Kayla closer to my side, "We're being followed. I don't like some of them; they're really creepy."

"I sense them as well," Kayla says, "Our presence and intention have drawn others to us. But they won't harm us; we are here in peace, at Hecate's request. And it's not our place to judge or reject those drawn to the healing magic of the Dark Goddess. She welcomes all, the living and the dead, and angels and demons."

In response to Kayla's words, something seems to settle in the liquid darkness, like a silent sigh that ripples through the dream landscape and widens the pathway before and behind us. With a loud, resonate bark from the lead dog, the bright flicker of a hearth fire appears several yards away.

We stop at the shadowed edge of the firelight. The space appears empty except for the scarlet and amber flames rising to lick the night sky. A base, primal rhythm pounds in my chest. I scent the air and discern faint traces of wild rose amidst the stronger smell of wood smoke. Hecate is here; I feel Her presence, but I can't see Her.

Kayla's lips are slightly parted and an intense heat rises from her skin.

"We've found Hecate's hearth fire," she says, her voice husky and eager, "Come, She is waiting for us."

I pause, my upper torso extending forward and the rest of me frozen in place. Do I want this? My heart quickens within the narrow confines of my ribcage. Yes, absolutely, I want this. But do I belong here? Will I be welcome?

A cold, wet nose plays against my open palm and I look down into the glowing-coal eyes of our star-browed dog companion. An understanding passes between us. The Dark Goddess mysteries are now open to me; I have earned this moment. An overwhelming relief floods through me as I pass from the darkness into the light of Hecate's realm, like a lost traveler who has finally found her way home.

In the middle of the hearth-fire circle, bent over and absorbed in Her task, Hecate stirs a steaming cauldron that hangs suspended over the crackling, hissing flames. Clack, clack, clack — the scarred wood of Her staff strikes the blackened iron pot as She mutters quietly under Her breath.

Her night-sky black cloak sparkles as She moves, as if it's been dusted with starlight. Hecate straightens up and pushes back unruly strands of silver hair. She seems ageless, or perhaps all ages at once, as Her face shifts form through the veil of wood smoke — sometimes a smooth-browed maiden, sometimes the rounded flesh of a mother, and sometimes the wrinkled folds of an ancient.

With a dancer's grace, Hecate turns and then takes each of us in with Her penetrating, amethyst eyes. A touch of mischief plays at the corners of Her mouth, softening, somewhat, the intensity of Her scrutiny. I stand absolutely still, keeping eye contact, but not daring to say a word. I feel Her awareness peeling away my outer layers, penetrating my sweating skin and cutting through to my very core.

Our exchange unclothes me, stripping me back to basics, with no masks or inner barriers separating us one from the other. No personal defect, secret shame or buried longing goes unheeded, nor any act of kindness, instance of joy or hidden beauty. I couldn't be more naked and exposed, but rather than unsettling me I feel centered and solid in my bones and flesh. Hecate smiles at me, warm, welcoming, and I smile in return.

"Mother," Kayla says, closing the distance between them, "You have called to us and we have come."

With a single finger, Hecate traces the fine-boned contours of Kayla's face as if to take in its cherished lines. Kayla kisses the center of Hecate's palm and nestles it against her cheek.

"So you have," Hecate says, Her voice strong and musical, like a mountain stream in spring flood, "You heeded my dream quest and braved my dogs, even you, Sarah, so new and untested in the ways of magic. My path has led you to my hearth fire and magic cauldron."

The blackened pot, as if on cue, bubbles up and releases gray tendrils of vapor.

"My magic is impatient," Hecate says, "Come, our time together is short. Tonight we will take a storytelling journey, one that returns to beginnings so that we may know our way forward. We will start with your story, Kayla. Do you remember when our journey together began?"

Kayla closes her eyes and rubs the heel of her hand across her mid-torso.

She is silent for a minute, her forehead creased in concentration, and then says, "You know, I don't really remember. When I started to read about the Goddess and do magic, it was always the Dark Goddess that spoke to me — Kali Ma, Ereshkigal and you, Hecate. Later it seemed as if you'd always been by my side, guiding my dreams and my travels. But I can't pinpoint a specific moment or event that began my journey work with you."

"Twenty-five years ago, on a Winter Solstice eve — with my powers palpable in the long, cold exhalation of the darkest night — you first found your way to my hearth-fire realm," Hecate says, "Look into my cauldron and remember."

A small disturbance begins to percolate in the cauldron's center and then spreads outward in concentric, aromatic rings. The smells bring to mind the fresh, icy snap of new-fallen snow. And then the images appear, transforming the watery surface into a moving-picture screen.

An expanse of windows frames the slow, swirling descent of crystalline snowflakes that transform the frozen, urban landscape into silent, white beauty. It is the dead of night and nothing moves under the parallel rows of street lights, save for fleeting sparkles momentarily caught in the fluorescent glare.

The scene pans inward to a bedroom that would be right at home in a modern-design magazine, with its stark, straight edges and minimalist ethos: white walls, black platform bed with white linens, built-in, black cabinets with silver hardware, and a thick, white area rug on black-stained wood floors. The only touch of decorative color is a framed print of a scarlet rosebud, not yet unfurled from its leafy green wrappings. Order prevails in the space. The surfaces are clear of debris, save for a single book on the nightstand and a charcoal suit jacket neatly draped over the back of a leather and stainless-steel chair. A cardboard box in the corner holds a cache of Christmas presents in pretty coats of metallic green, red and gold wrapping paper.

The one exception to this serene, immaculate environment is the golden-haired, sleeping woman. Her body is contracted into a tight ball, with her knees close to her chest and her arms curved protectively over the top of her head. The duvet lies in a crumpled heap around her feet, half on the bed and half on the floor. As we watch, her face muscles twitch and work themselves into a scowl. Even with this distortion, I can see that this is a younger Kayla from the same pleasing lines of her cheekbones, nose and lips, and the small mole on the left side of her chin.

The vision zooms in on young Kayla's mid-brow, and then we are inside her head, witnessing the disturbing dream written so plainly on her sleeping face. For a second, this abrupt change in perspective disorients me, but my eyes adjust to the dim, murky light and I see young Kayla wandering in a dingy maze of backstreet alleys. Graffiti-scarred brick walls enclose her on either side as she fumbles her way through endless, monotonous twists and turns. Her breath is quick and shallow and her wide eyes dart from side to side, like those of a hunted animal.

Snarling, demon-like voices nip at her heels, "You better get going on that new client presentation. You've barely looked at it and the whole thing is way over your head. John doesn't like you. He's sure to trip you up. You'd better be perfect, don't screw up like last time. Your father is going to really hate those leather gloves you bought him. And perfume for your sister? Again? When was the last time you went to the gym? Did you notice the jiggling fat on your thighs? No Christmas treats for you . . ." On and on the voices drone, voraciously buzzing around her, like mosquitoes after blood.

In the spaces between the words, other voices whisper a counter-melody message, "This is your life, Kayla — all that really matters — all you'll ever deserve — you'll never get out of this twisted maze — we won't let you go — there is no escape."

I don't want to hear these voices. I don't want to hear them! I push the heels of my hands hard against my ears. But I can't block them out. They're inside my head too, "What are you doing here? Have you lost your mind? Marsha and Trent are sabotaging your career but good. Matt covering your back, you've got to be kidding! Trent is going to be doing his victory crow before the year is out. What kind of a friend are you, sending Jules to do your dirty work? She could have been caught, fired, while you're off playing in la la land, leaving your Opa alone on his deathbed. Get a grip. Get on that plane tomorrow. Forget this ever happened . . ."

Young Kayla stops still and sniffs the air. There's a breeze that wasn't there before, lightly blowing back her disheveled hair and clearing the stale, fetid air. Her scowl fades and the hunted look leaves her eyes.

"You lie!" she says, "There is a way out of here. This is my life! Mine! And I'm not going to listen to you anymore!"

I gasp and drop my hands from my ears. Yes! Yes! You lie, you demon bastards! Get out of my head! Get out of my life!

The demons are silent; the twisted maze of backstreet alleys is gone. Another voice arises in this empty space, with rich, compelling, feminine tones that squeeze my heart tight with yearning. Whether this voice emerges from young Kayla's dream, from my inner depth or from the midnight folds of the Winter Solstice magic, I cannot tell.

"I am waiting for you, sweet one," She calls out softly, "Come, it is time. You are ready, you are ripe."

"Mother! Mother! I don't know where you are?" young Kayla cries out, "I need you! Help me, please help me!"

At her feet a path materializes, hewn of red granite paving stones, flecked with tiny glimmers of silver light; it's the very same path that led us to Hecate's hearth fire. In the far distance, scarlet and amber flames dance in a freshening wind that carries the smoky scent of burning wood resin.

The dream vision fades and I am staring into the flat, reflective plane of the cauldron surface. It mirrors back Kayla and my merged reflections, fusing together, in my mind, her past with my present.

"This is not just Kayla's story," I say, turning to Hecate, "It's mine as well."

Hecate touches me, placing Her forehead lightly against mine. I take in Her scent of bruised sage and wild roses, filling my lungs and imprinting Her unique fragrance onto my sensual memory bank.

"You see clearly, Sarah," Hecate says, "The surface details differ, but you and Kayla share the same deep story — the tale of my lost daughter who heeds the call of her aching soul and finds her way back to my living realm and ways. Nothing is lost that cannot be refound. New beginnings emerge from the darkest night of the soul."

"I have no memory of this dream," Kayla says, "I didn't

know about magic or dreams back then. I didn't even know that I was unhappy. How could this have been when we started our work together?"

"Think back," Hecate says, "And the truth will come to you."

Again Kayla turns her gaze inward and rubs her belly region, as if her lost memories reside there.

"Oh yes, yes," Kayla says, "That winter there was tons of snow. A few months after Christmas, I had a ski accident that fractured my skull. It put me out of commission for several months, and when I returned to work I knew I hated my job and had to leave. By September I was working at another company and, out of nowhere, I became interested in spirituality."

"Your dream led you to my hearth fire on that Winter Solstice," Hecate says, "and my cauldron shared its storytelling magic. It showed you another way, my path, the Path of She. Though you woke from the dream remembering nothing, still your life was set on a new course. Your accident began your waking world travels with me."

"And I've been journeying with you ever since," Kayla says.

"Yes, Kayla," Hecate says, "You and I have come full circle and a new beginning is upon us. It is time for my path to re-emerge in the waking world, and I need you to be a SheBard, a priestess and teacher of my ways. You know my Path of She in your body and soul because you have spent half your life walking its mysteries. Now I'm asking you to look into my cauldron and retrace your steps so we can move forward together."

A shadow passes over Kayla's face that clouds her eyes and drags down the corners of her mouth, revealing a profound vulnerability and sadness that I'd never noticed before. Hecate takes Kayla into Her arms and they gently sway together, a Mother and daughter sharing breath, heartbeats and a deep grief that I don't yet understand.

"It is time," Hecate says to Kayla, "You are ready, you are ripe."

I feel the throbbing of my soul, cocooned within the shining ember in my solar plexus, and I reach out, hungrily, to touch Hecate's and Kayla's backs.

"I want to look into your cauldron," I say, "I want to travel your Path of She."

Hecate and Kayla turn to me, wiping tears from their eyes and laughing softly.

"Yes, Sarah, that is why you are here," Hecate says, "I will show you my Path of She. You are meant to journey by Kayla's side and help bring fresh eyes to these ancient ways."

Clack, clack, clack — Hecate takes up Her wooden staff and stirs Her cauldron brew. The flames rise higher, caressing the contours of the burnt, black metal, and the inky liquid begins to boil and steam. A tug in my mid-torso pulls me to Hecate's side and compels my gaze downward. Kayla stands across from me, seemingly equally transfixed.

"This is my storytelling brew," Hecate intones, "It holds the tales of what was, what is and what shall be — from the first stirrings of life in the far distant past, to the unformed possibilities of the far distant future. To know my Path of She, you must seek out the four master tales, each a chapter in the unfolding of humanity and a gateway into the lost fragments of your whole, holy self. These are original stories, the lost Tales of She, before they were distorted and erased from your human knowing. Let us begin at the very beginning."

Hecate bends low and whispers into the cauldron's watery depth, "Show us the Tale of Creation."

The dark brew stills to reveal a vast, pulsing blackness that explodes into infinite fragments of radiant starlight. Spiral arrays of swirling bits of fiery debris spread outward. Chunks of stellar rubble collide and coalesce into flaming balls of light. A molten-lava landscape belches out gaseous clouds of muggy vapor and red liquid matter that cools and hardens to moon-bare bedrock. A shift in perspective takes us inside the silver, shimmering slime of a primeval sea where tiny amoebic life forms quiver and divide. Faster and faster images fly by, taking us in mere minutes from single-celled creatures to the fleshed complexities of plants, fish, reptiles, birds and mammals.

Ecstatic waves of energy ripple through the master tale's visions and infuse my every molecule with fiery passion. Hecate's throaty moans, Kayla's heavy, steamy breath become my own. I lose sense of where their minds and musculature end and mine begin. Our hips arch forward and back, forward and back, as if a Cosmic God makes love to us.

A last bubble rises up and unfolds into the naked, olive-skinned forms of a man and a woman. They stand upright, hand-in-hand, and soft streams of light shine forth from their genitals, their hearts and the crown of their heads. The image offers up its beauty for a brief second and then breaks apart into an iridescent bank of mist.

The distinct boundaries of my own mind and body return. I press my palms over my fast-beating heart and take in the hot pounding of my blood and the rapturous firing of my nerve endings. A luscious satisfaction spreads from my sex and infuses me, from the top of my head to the soles of my feet.

Hecate passes Her right hand through the iridescent mist, gathering up musky droplets of condensation. Her fingers curl into a tight fist and then uncurl to reveal a single, jet black seed.

She presses the seed to Her lips, her eyes dreamy and seemingly lost in the afterglow of love making.

"This is the story seed of the master Tale of Creation," Hecate says, "Of all the lost stories, it is the one I grieve the most. With its loss, you have forgotten the deepest, most exquisite parts of your human nature: that you were conceived, like all of Creation, from the ecstatic coupling of light and matter, and of God and Goddess; that love, the primal desire to create and nurture new life, is the very base of your essence; and that each of you has your own unique fragment of the Cosmos in your starlit core. These are the gifts that life has granted you and that you have squandered."

The delicious heat leaves my body and I clutch at the power place in my solar plexus.

"These things aren't really lost are they?" I say, "I mean, can't we get this part of ourselves back? I've seen this starlight inside of me. It has woken up, at least that's what it feels like to me. Doesn't that change things?"

"Yes, Sarah," Hecate says, "It changes everything. You can never lose the beauty that you are. You have to find it again, like you have done, and then embrace the hard task of returning your Divine core to the center of your life. This is the journey work of the black seed. But we must move on; the next tale awaits us."

Hecate stirs the brew counterclockwise until the mist of the Tale of Creation is drawn downward and disappears into the cauldron's belly. Kayla shakes her body and I do the same, emptying ourselves of one story in readiness for the next.

When the surface stills, Hecate bends low and whispers, "Show us the Tale of the Garden."

Lush, ripe wafts rise up from the cauldron in sensuous, steamy tendrils and then unfurl into a scene of a verdant, untouched paradise. A grove of swaying sycamores gives way to thickets of berry-laden bushes and a sun-dappled meadow painted with wildflower splashes of purple and yellow. The burbling of a nearby stream tumbles amidst the delicate treble of birdsong and the distant, full-throated howl of a wild dog sounding its pack.

A raven-haired maiden, with eyes as green as the meadow grass, lies on her belly in the sunlit center of this landscape, seemingly entranced by the antics of a honeybee as it dips in and out of mauve clover. A buzzing hums in her throat in perfect mimicry of her insect companion. The sound of her bee voice fills me up, tuning me into the young woman's sensual communion with the bee's reality, so like my joining with the raven on Mount Maxwell.

As the creature collects its flower treasures, a visceral understanding of its essence passes from bee to woman to me: the taste of nectar gathered on outstretched tongue, the cloying grasp of pollen on fine leg hairs and the whole-body thrum of beating wings. The connection stretches and then severs as the bee flies away. With closed eyes, the woman touches two fingers to her brow, and I share her deep reverence and tingling delight.

A low, husky voice calls from the forest edge. The maiden leaps up, as lithe as a deer, and bounds into her man's naked embrace. He has dark hair, olive skin and hazel eyes with speckles of copper in a field of sage green. His lips seek out hers and I feel their warm, velvety caress on my lips. They share a lingering kiss that tastes of the tart currants that stain his mouth crimson and the salt of his sweat. Their consciousness co-mingles, though not as completely as woman and bee. In their touching, I sense a rippling forth of silver strands of light that synchronize their cadence of nerve, heart and breath, and that radiate outward to the earth, the heavens and the wild otherness of this stunning world.

This delicious, silver-threaded connection feels familiar — yes, yes — it's the same as my flight with the raven — and, mmmm, yes, also my kiss with Will.

The man and maiden are entwined as the vision dissolves into honeysuckle-scented vapors. The sensual imprint of her body knowing on mine and the soft, damp impression of her man's lips are gone. And I feel hollow, like someone has pulled out the best parts of my stuffing and left an empty shell behind.

With a sweep of Her fingertips, Hecate collects the strands of sweet vapors and compresses them into a lily white seed.

"This is the story seed of the master Tale of the Garden," She says, "It shares with us the first turning of humanity when the world was young and fresh. Your primeval ancestors walked the earth at one with the Divine spark shining in their core and the sensuous powers of their living bodies. Goddess, Mother, Holy One — it was I who watched over and guided my human children, teaching them to honor the ways and mysteries of the wild earth. And it was they who delighted me, and their Godly Father, by giving voice and new forms to the earth's wonders."

I lock onto the lily white seed in Hecate's cupped palm. I want this Garden seed world that Hecate has shown Kayla and me. I want to be whole, at one with the powers of my starlit core and earth-made body, like the raven-haired, green-eyed maiden. I want every kiss to taste like tart currants and the salt on my lover's skin. I want to fly with ravens and gather nectar with bees. I want these things that I never knew were possible before I came to Salt Spring. I want them, even though they scare the hell out of me.

"But how, Hecate, how did we lose such a precious part of our humanity?" I ask, unable to keep the pleading note out of my voice.

Kayla's shoulders tighten and the shadow of sadness distorts her features once more. A chill passes through my center; Kayla already knows the answer to this question, and it isn't good.

"Everything has its natural cycles," Hecate says, "Long did my human children follow my ways and those of your original ancestors. My daughters wore the red cloak of priestess and my sons worked to serve community and the powers of life. But as day turns to night, and life to decay, so too the good dream of humanity had its time in the sunlight, only to be eclipsed by the bad dream of its shadow side. This is our next master tale."

Hecate takes up Her staff and whisks down the sweet, floral fragrance of the Tale of the Garden into the cauldron's depth.

When the surface stills, She bends low and whispers, "Show us the Tale of the Fall."

The liquid roils, belching out a wretched stench that conjures up images of diseased bodies and childhood memories of my lonely, loveless home. My hands instinctively shield my face and my chest curves inward to guard my tender heart.

"Do not close down," Hecate says, "These stories are part of your humanity. Their truths are essential for your healing and return to wholeness. Trust in your courage and your strength to follow where my magic leads you."

One glance at Kayla makes me brave. Her face is grim, but her back is straight and her steady gaze remains fixed on the cauldron's surface. She has not shut down and neither will I.

Ruthlessly, in rapid, overlapping images, the cauldron blazes with a horrifying collage that lays bare the vilest elements of our human history: rotting corpses of red-robed women amidst the smashed destruction of their sanctuary; weeping, sooty faces of villagers watching their thatched homes and crop lands burn; carrion birds converging on a battlefield strewn with the massacred bodies of men; a woman spread-legged and vacant as a rutting conqueror claims his victory rights; an adolescent boy dressed as a soldier, with a gore-smeared sword and a look of white-faced terror. On and on the scenes play out, each as devastating as the last.

My muscles constrict in my buttocks, gut and chest, cold and rigid, like metal exposed to harsh, winter elements. But I don't look away. I can't look away.

The frame shifts to modern times and images familiar to me: the shadows of the dead on the walls of Hiroshima, left behind by those instantly vaporized by the heat of the atomic blast; the Vietnam Memorial Wall in Washington, a gravestone longer than a football field and almost twice my height at its apex, carved with the names of the slaughtered youth from a brutal, senseless war; an aerial view of the deforestation of the Amazon rainforest, with an advancing line of raging fires cutting the landscape in two: one side jungle green wilderness, the other a wasteland of charred stumps; and a prostitute leaning against a doorjamb in downtown Toronto, a girl, not much past sixteen, with a hollow, blank stare and bubblegum pink lipstick.

A burning shame mixes with my horror. There is no hiding here from the raw ugliness of my humanity. I clamp my hand over my mouth, trying to stifle a building retch.

The cauldron offers up a final vision of an old bag lady wearing dirty, black rags, with rotten teeth and dull eyes that flash with madness and hate. She mutters to herself as she digs around in her garbage-filled grocery cart. I can just make out the broken shards of a Venus figurine, a half-eaten apple and the tattered remains of a red cloak. With a sickening squelch, the cauldron swallows this hag woman whole and leaves behind a host of spectral demons and ghosts hovering within the smoky, toxic fumes of this master tale.

Hecate is as motionless as a statue, Her hands folded in prayer over Her breastbone and Her head bowed in silence.

The misty demons and ghosts kiss the hem of Her cloak and then slip into the space between Her pressed palms. When they are all gone, She extends Her arms and opens Her hands; a blood red seed rests within their cupped interior.

My feet are rooted to the spot and my body is locked up tight. I want to back away from this red story seed and retreat into the not-me place inside my mind that can shield me from these dreadful visions. I want to scream and cry and vomit out everything I've taken in. Kayla moves beside me and slips her arm around my waist, and I cling to the warm touch of her body against mine.

Hecate's eyes are on us — not eyes tinged with madness, like the hag in the cauldron, nor hateful, judging eyes that reflect back my shame and fear of my humanity — but compassionate, kind eyes, the eyes of a Mother who still loves Her children, no matter the bad deeds that they have done.

"This is the story seed of the master Tale of the Fall," She says, "It reveals the second turning of humanity, and your descent from the good dream of your ancient ancestors into the bad dream of the worst instincts of your nature. My cauldron has given you but a small taste of the harm that your species has done to me, to the Mother Earth and to each other.

"I see and name the terrible truths of the red-seed times, but I do not judge or condemn you. To find out who they truly are, children must try their strength and test their limits outside of the protecting arms and defining ways of their Mother. Your fall from the Garden and your rejection of my mysteries are natural steps in coming into your full maturity.

"It has been my hardest, most grievous task to stand back and let you find your own way, knowing that I could not protect you from the polarities of your nature. For your kind has been blessed and cursed with the dual powers of creation and destruction, and the free will to choose whether to live by the laws of love or dominion. You chose destruction, dominion and fear, and your beast nature over your beauty."

The sadness hasn't lifted from Kayla's face, but she nods as Hecate speaks and then says, "We lost you and our best nature so we could choose again. Like the Winter Solstice, the new dawn is born from the darkest night."

I push away from Kayla and stand apart from both of them. My stomach is cramped and my chest is heaving. How can Hecate still love us and justify what we've done? And how can Kayla so calmly accept everything we've been shown?

"What are you two talking about?" I say, "There is nothing redeemable about those things we saw in the cauldron. Nothing! We are monsters with thousands of years of murder, rape and endless suffering under our belt. And, goddamn us, it's not really any different now. We still murder and rape and treat each other like dirt. And then pretend nothing is wrong. We took your beauty, Hecate, and the gifts you gave us, and made you into that hag."

"There are so many other things my cauldron could have shown you," Hecate says gently, "Life doesn't divide so easily along lines of good and evil, and beauty and beast, but is made of a complex weaving of all these qualities. Humanity's better instincts are still very much present in the world. Acts of horror are balanced with acts of kindness, destructive forces with creative impulses, and hatred and bigotry with love and compassion.

"I am asking much of you this eve, Sarah. These things are not so new and raw for Kayla, for she has been traveling my ways for many years. My Path of She is not for the faint of heart. You must journey into the darkest places of your soul and your humanity. But you do so knowing the master Tales of Creation and the Garden, and their wisdom teachings of the Divine roots and true, best qualities of your humanity.

"The master Tale of the Fall also offers a wisdom teaching: everything that unfolds in matter has a purpose, even the worst of these red-seed tales of horror. Like a pearl born of the chafing of grit, you come into your full beauty and power through the chafing of life. The invitation for healing and profound change most often lies in your suffering. Open your heart and see if my words ring true."

I place my hands on my heart — breathe in, breathe out, breathe in, breathe out — my Opa Kass comes to me. His life has been terrible in ways I cannot imagine. He grew up in Nazi Germany. He never talks about it, but he must have seen the worst atrocities of humanity up close. And he had so much heartbreak of his own, as an immigrant to the United States when Germans were hated, losing the young wife he adored, and then my dad, his only child, dying before they had a chance to reconcile their differences. Yet my Opa is the most loving, beautiful person I know. Somehow his hardships made him shine brighter and love life, and me, more.

All my life he has been teaching me about Hecate's middle path, where joy dances with pain, and death with life. The dog-man's words come back to me, "Must be big. Big like world. Big like the Mother." Big like my Opa Kass.

Though I feel like I'm going to be sick, I say, "Yes, Hecate, your words ring true."

"Then we must move on to the last master tale," Hecate says, "It too will challenge you, Sarah, and you, Kayla, but I ask you both to stay present and open to its teachings."

Kayla reaches for my hand and together we return to the edge of Hecate's blackened iron pot.

Hecate grasps Her gnarled staff and stirs.

"Humanity hovers on the cusp of the third turning, the Great Turning," She says, "You have come to the end of one cycle and balance precariously on an evolutionary edge. This last master tale is only beginning. It is woven of the lived stories of individual souls who embrace the transformative magic of their beauty and their wounding. And it is this magic that can turn the tides of humanity's downward, destructive spiral and return you to the good dream of my life serving ways."

The magic brew shifts from a murky gray to a velvety, midnight black. The surface stills and then Hecate bends low and whispers, "Show us the Tale of the Shining."

The cauldron surface fills with the lovely visage of a little girl with white blonde locks, sparkling, violet blue eyes and a beaming, contagious grin that reminds me of my new friend Emilie.

I feel Kayla's arm tense before she drops my hand.

"That's me when I was three, just before my abuse started," she says, "Why are you showing us this, Hecate?"

Hecate draws Kayla close and touches her brow to brow.

She speaks in a low voice, perhaps only for Kayla's ears and heart, "I could not spare you the pain of your childhood and I cannot spare you your pain now. My cauldron shares your childhood story because it holds the transformative magic of the Tale of the Shining. We have traveled this long, hard road together, my daughter, and now we are nearing its end. I ask you to trust me and to let your story guide you and Sarah in the mysteries of the Shining."

Kayla's body is rigid and trembling. She takes several long, unsteady breaths, and then, almost imperceptibly, nods her head.

"Yes," Kayla says, "Yes, I am ready."

This time it is me who reaches for Kayla's hand.

The vision of little Kayla's face begins to transform, crumpling in on itself as she scrunches her eyes closed and clamps her mouth in a taut, white grimace. A man kneels behind her, clutching her naked hips, pumping his poison into her tiny body cavity, and ripping her in two with his adult, hard maleness. Whimpers and squeaks escape from between her clenched teeth.

"Shut up, you fucking, whining slut," he grunts, digging his dirty fingers into her tender babe skin.

After a couple more brutal thrusts, he finishes his business with a harsh moan. The cauldron vapors reek with the rancid stench of his unwashed body and the curdled amalgam of his ejaculate and her blood. He roughly pushes her away and then laughs as she buries her face in the pillow and sobs.

I start to shake uncontrollably, tears streaming down my face. Kayla's hand squeezes mine so hard, I feel my bones crushing together.

More heart-wrenching images flash by. He repeatedly rapes her, not as random, disconnected acts, but with an apparent intent to break her spirit: in the dark of night, his hand clamped over her mouth and the house filled with the muffled snores of those who could protect her; at the shadowy back of the garage, her face pushed down amongst the stinking garbage cans; and in her little bed, with a circle of her stuffed animals watching from the sunlit dresser.

Every desecrating act is punctuated with mind-fuck, foul talk: "No one loves you. No one will protect you. If your daddy finds out, he'll do this to you too"; "Bend over and take it. You like it. You ask for it. You want more"; "You're a worthless whore. A dirty, bad girl. A piece of dog shit."

The surface returns to an image of Kayla's little-girl face, splotched and bloated, with eyes dull and guarded; there is no grin, no spark and no life.

Shock waves rivet through my body, flooding my limbs with grief and rage.

"That bastard! That fucking monster!" I say, and then grab Kayla into a tight, tight hug, "How can you bear this, Kayla? How? How?"

Despite these terrible, terrible images from her childhood, it's Kayla who comforts me.

She wraps me in her arms, strokes my hair and says, "It's okay, Sarah, it's okay. He can't hurt me anymore. I'm too strong now. I'm strong."

And in her strong arms, I let myself cry for the horrible things that Hecate's cauldron has shown us, for the unspeakable abomination Kayla has suffered, and for the pain in my heart and the pain in this world.

For a long time we hold each other, with Hecate crooning softly and encircling us in Her comforting embrace. When we break apart, Kayla takes my wet cheeks in her hands and gifts me with a warm, tender smile, all the more poignant against the profound sadness in her eyes that I suspect neither time nor healing will ever completely mend.

Hecate guides us back to face the cauldron, "The storytelling is not done. There is one more vision I would share ere this night is done."

With a noisy sniff, I take in a brightening, fragrant shift in the rising steam that now offers up the heady scents of a spring garden in full bloom. The watery surface opens onto a scene of a smiling, slightly older, little Kayla, with grass-stained knees poking out beneath the hem of a blue, floral-print cotton shift. She wanders amidst the meandering border plantings of snow white peonies, deep purple irises, fire red poppies and a seemingly endless profusion of pretty-faced flowers.

Her tongue protrudes slightly from her lips, her face a mask of quiet concentration, as she selects and arranges blooms in a white plastic flower bowl. As a finishing touch, she inserts a smattering of wild lily of the valley, picked from the ditch at the side of the property. Their teeny, perfect, white bells and slender, green stalks offer a playful contrast to the cultivated loveliness of their domestic sisters. She carries her bouquet into the house, places it in the center of a scuffed, wooden table and then basks in her mother's red-lipstick smile.

"I loved making those flower arrangements for my mom," Kayla says, reaching out as if to touch the child in the vision.

Little Kayla turns toward us and reaches back with her small, delicate hand. Their fingers entwine amidst the shifting vapors, and then she is gone, slipping silently back into the bubbling, watery depth. A single, golden tear slides down Kayla's cheek, splashes just inside the iron rim, and sets off a ripple that spirals sunwise into the swallowing center of the cauldron's belly.

Hecate passes her hand through the aromatic steam and captures a smooth-skinned, gold seed that shines with an inner luminescence.

"This story seed contains the formative elements of the master Tale of the Shining," She says, "As a young child, Kayla, you already carried the alchemy of the gold seed. In your flesh and bones, you bore the best and the worst of humanity: the gaping wound of rape and the undimmed beauty of a child's loving heart.

"What the Tale of the Shining asks of you, Kayla, it asks of all my waking children: to become powerful enough, wise enough and big enough to accept all that you are and to push nothing away. You must become the crucible that holds the truth and the tension inherent in your life story — the horror and the joy, and the beauty and the wounding — and let what wants to be born in you, be born.

"This is the alchemical magic of the Shining, not only for you, Kayla, but for you also, Sarah, and for anyone who finds their way to my Path of She."

"But why does it have to be so hard, so painful?" I say, "Kayla's childhood abuse, losing my Opa Kass and the terrible things we've seen in your cauldron — why does it have to hurt so badly for us to change?"

"There is no easy answer to your question. Humanity is part of the great unfolding Universe and, like all of creation, your evolution is driven by the collision of opposites. Within your inner landscape, you hold the opposing energies of the good dream of the Garden and the bad dream of the Fall, and the light and shadow inherent in your nature. With collision comes awareness of polarities, with awareness comes conscious choice, and with conscious choice you can heal and transform your life and your world. What has been lost can be refound, all the more cherished than if it had never been lost at all."

"This is what Ereshkigal showed us at the Winter Solstice ritual, Sarah," Kayla says, "We can't reclaim our beauty without embracing our wounding, and together they make the dirt of life brew that can return the Goddess and our best nature to the waking world. It was your brew that kissed Inanna back to life."

I put my fingers to my mouth; I can still sense Inanna's lifeless, ruby lips against mine, and my sweet, slow embrace of my feminine soul, both the awakening kiss of a sleeping beauty. I place a single finger against Kayla's lips and feel the alive, warm movement of her breath.

Black, white and red vapors rise from Hecate's storytelling cauldron. Where they meet and intertwine, golden light shines outward and fills the room with a luminescent force that pushes against my breastbone and then passes through the outer barrier of my skin into the inner lattice of my being.

I place my hands in a prayer position against the quivering spot where this force entered my body, and when I open my palms four seeds rest within their cupped interior: one jet black, one lily white, one blood red and one shiny gold. Beside me Kayla also holds four seeds.

"So without, so within," Hecate says, "You are not separate from my cauldron's master tales; their essences echo within you — four lost Tales of She, four lost elements of your whole, holy self, held within the black, white, red and gold story seeds.

"The Tales of She have no power on their own. You must choose to open your hearts and knowing to their mysteries. You must decide whether you are ready to follow where they lead, and to play your part in returning my ways to the waking world. My time has come again and together we can rise from the ashes and begin anew."

Four seeds, pulsing and warm, like living flesh pressed up against my living skin — if I say yes, where will they lead me? To the star-bright fragment of the Cosmos pulsing in my core? To the ancient, wild part of me that is so intensely, sensually alive? To her wounded twin cowering in the shadowy recesses of my psyche? To the transformative powers of my life story?

I search Kayla's face, looking for direction. I know now the hard path she has traveled to become such a powerful woman, and the horror she endured as a child that was the price of the immensity of her spirit. What am I willing to endure to follow Hecate's Path of She?

Within my cupped palms and trembling heart I hold my destiny. I can risk what I've got and move past my fears into the vast potential of my true, deep self. I can choose to follow

Hecate's ancient path and let its mysteries heal my life and my world. I can become Hecate's daughter, no longer lost, but returned to Her powers and ways.

I exhale a breath that I didn't know I was holding. A joy rush begins in my core and surges upward, lighting up my face with a mischievous grin.

And then I ask Kayla the life-changing question she has put to me twice before, "Are you in?"

"Yes," she says, returning my grin, "Absolutely, yes!"

As the first shining rays of the dawn brush away the ebony tarp of night, the four seeds pass by our parted lips. I run my damp tongue over their smooth surfaces and then track their tingling passage into my gestating interior. A heat rises in my core as my juices break down the barriers between the seeds' essences and my own.

"So it is chosen, so it will be!" Hecate proclaims, ringing ours vows outward into the listening Universe.

The fading night bursts into a million golden stars. Hecate, Her hearth fire and Her cauldron are gone, and I am once again sitting across from Kayla on a cushion in her meditation room, with the blissful snores of Shire rumbling from a darkened corner.

CHAPTER 8

EVERYDAY MAGIC

Pebble-sized raindrops pound against the windowpanes
and beat out their rhythmic presence on the metal roof.
The smell of pancakes and brewing coffee lure me into Kayla's
kitchen, dressed in the red fleece housecoat she loaned to me.
Our ritual ended in the wee hours of the night and I couldn't
manage the drive back to my hotel.

Cheery warmth emanates from the stove, pushing back the
oppressive gloom of the charcoal-bellied clouds that glower
down at us through the windows. Like the rest of the house, the
kitchen is decorated in an earthier version of modern design:
umber walls, clean-lined walnut cabinets, chocolate brown
granite counters with swirls of copper and black, and the latest
in stainless-steel appliances. French doors lead to a flagstone
patio with an outdoor eating area and pots of rosemary, thyme
and other herbs.

I scan Kayla's eyes and the lines of her face for tension and
grief, anything that mirrors the pain of Hecate's cauldron
visions. I can't tell whether the sadness I detect is hers or
my own projected outward. She smiles as she sets a plate of
blueberry pancakes in front of me and then starts into her
breakfast. I read her body language as eat first, talk later.

The hard seat of the wooden stool presses into my sore

bottom. My shoulders and limbs are cramped and tender and my mid-torso feels slightly bruised, like I've completed a triathlon rather than spent hours in the dream world. I eat slowly and my mouth registers nuances of texture and taste: the grainy bite of cornmeal in the batter, the gooey burst of tangy blueberries and the silky sweetness of maple syrup.

A repetitive click, click, click draws my attention to the wall clock; it's 8:30 and almost time for me to return to my hotel to pack. My floatplane leaves at noon and my flight back to Toronto is at 2:30. And then what? No Kayla, no Emilie, no Will and no Salt Spring magical community. No fresh, crisp air, no towering evergreen trees, no black-green ocean, no mountain views and no ethereal mists. Back to Marsha and Trent, and whatever maelstrom Matt has brewed in my absence. Back to the close, smelly press of subway commutes, the grinding routine of sixty-hour work weeks and solitary meals eaten on the fly. Back to a world with no magic and no one to travel with on Hecate's path, let alone understand what I've experienced here. And soon Opa Kass will be gone and I'll truly be alone.

"So we're locked into the Path of She, aren't we?" I ask as I begin to gather up our breakfast dishes.

"I'd say so," Kayla says, "Swallowing those seeds sealed our magic. When you make a vow to Hecate, She holds you to it."

We wash the dishes side by side in a companionable silence. I relax into the mundane familiarity of the lemon-scented dish soap, the hot water against my skin and the clink of china against china.

"Four master tales and four lost parts of myself," I say after putting away the final dish, "I don't have a clue what any of this means, and I'm going to be by myself in Toronto, with no one to help me figure these things out."

"Think of the magic you've already experienced without

any help," Kayla says, leaning against the granite countertop, "And how present and powerful you've been in our ritual work. You've proven yourself to be a person of power, Sarah, with great courage and natural magical abilities. Trust yourself. Trust me. Trust Hecate. We don't need to know what it all means, just that there is a path and I've traveled it before."

I stand across from Kayla, with the warm stove to my back and the French doors to my right. The dense fir trees stand still in the windless air, their branches soaked from this morning's deluge. A deer sticks its nose into one of the herb pots, not more than ten feet from the door, seemingly indifferent to human artifacts like a house and patio furniture.

Trust, damn, that's never been one of my favorite words, nor do I like traveling by the seat of my pants. I operate better with goals, agendas and to do lists; things you can plan for, implement and then check off once they're done.

"But what am I supposed to do?" I say, "What comes next?"

"I know this must be hard for you," Kayla says, "I'm also from the corporate world where everything seems concrete and laid out. But magic only works when you don't try to constrain it with preset outcomes and destinations. We're looking for what has been lost, not what we already know. To do that, we have to trust the journey itself, and where our lives and magic lead us."

"Even when they unearth the ugliness and pain the cauldron showed us?" I say, "Your childhood abuse was so horrible, Kayla. Are you really okay with all of this?"

The sadness is there; it descends, like a storm cloud, and shifts the contours of Kayla's features. But it doesn't appear to deflate or consume her. Her gaze is direct and unflinching, and her voice as steady and potent as ever.

"I won't pretend that my childhood wasn't devastating," Kayla says, "or that it wasn't painful to relive my sexual abuse last night. But I accept my past completely. Where we find our wounding, we also find our beauty; I wouldn't be who I am now without these experiences. As Hecate said, it's the chafing of life that yields the pearl of our true beauty and power."

"My parents pretty much ignored me when I was growing up, and my dad died when I was a teenager," I say, and feel a storm cloud descend over my face.

Unbidden memories flash through my mind: of me as a toddler, my hands and nose pressed against the window, watching my parents' departing backs as they take off for a cruise and leave me with the nanny; of me barely past puberty, my eyes downcast and my cheeks burning red, buying sanitary pads at the drugstore; and of me as a teenager at my father's funeral, dry-eyed and empty. My mother and father never hugged or kissed me, rarely included me in their vacations and social life, and left me to navigate my girlhood transitions on my own. Only Opa Kass made things better and he won't be with me much longer.

A cold, hard resistance, like a thick plate-glass wall, divides my mind in half, with my conscious awareness on one side and these memories on the other. Don't feel it. Don't remember it. Then it can't hurt you.

"I don't want to deal with this stuff," I say, rubbing the aching spot in the middle of my forehead.

"The bad things don't go away," Kayla says, keeping her steady focus on me, "They're like tin cans tied to our tail. No matter how fast we run, they rattle away behind us, constantly disturbing our peace. My childhood abuse made me sick. I repressed my rape memories at an early age, but even though I had forgotten them, they didn't stop hurting me. I was numb and dead inside, and living a life that didn't feed my soul or make me happy. When you dim the pain, you also dim the joy."

My shopping gluttony, non-stop work and insubstantial love relationships — am I also sick inside? How much of my childhood neglect do I drag around like tin cans tied to my tail? Something is wrong with my life; my Salt Spring magic has recovered the lost part of my feminine soul, but there's more. Stuff has been creeping out of the shadows ever since I had that emotional breakdown in my office on Friday.

"Can Hecate's path really help us heal our childhood pain?" I say, "Can we ever truly move on from our past?"

"Yes," Kayla says, "Absolutely. I'm living proof of that."

"Of course, Kayla, of course," I say, "God, I'm so sorry! Here I am being a coward about my childhood when what happened to you was much worse."

"No, no, Sarah," Kayla says, coming close and taking my hands in hers, "We each have our pain to deal with. My parents have always loved and supported me. And my abuser was only in my life for six months. I wasn't neglected like you were. Who can say which harm is the greater? And there is no real value in comparing. You have your story and I have mine. We're meant to work with the material we're given.

"But it's not all doom and gloom. Remember the black and white seed master tales. We heal and reclaim our power and beauty, as well as our pain and wounding."

My hands gravitate to my mid-body; I feel the radiant heat and power of my starlit center and feminine soul. I have already begun this work. Whatever is deep and best within me has woken up. And that alone is worth the price of admission.

The rain has ceased its hammering on the roof and a weak sun leaks a few feeble rays through the dense, bleak cloud cover. The clock ticks, irrevocably drawing my time on Salt Spring to a close. I press Kayla's warm palm to my cheek and close my eyes.

"I don't want to go home," I say, "I don't want to deal with my job, my Opa Kass's illness and all this change by myself."

"After the ritual is done, the real work begins," Kayla says, standing back from me but still holding my hand, "You need to go home, Sarah. Your everyday life is your teacher and guide. The magic is there. Your journey work is there. You've made your vow to walk Hecate's path, and now your job is to pay attention and do the work that presents itself, whether it is lovely or nasty."

"When you say yes, change will come," I say.

"Exactly," Kayla says with a wide smile, "And you won't be alone. I have promised to be a SheBard for Hecate and to find the four master tales. We are traveling this road together. I will be there in any way you need me and I know you will be there for me as well. Hecate will be by our side, guiding us and sending allies and help when we need it."

"Like the raven," I say.

"Yes," Kayla says, "There is a whole magical world everywhere around you hidden in plain view, waiting to support your journey work."

A few short days ago, I wouldn't have believed a word of this. But I'm not that person anymore. I can't deny what I've experienced. I now know that magic is real and that there is another wild, delicious, terrifying reality just below the surface of the waking world.

"Can I come back and visit you on Salt Spring?" I ask.

"Absolutely," Kayla says, "Our adventure together has just begun."

Then we hug, a tight, bone-crunching hug, and I never, ever want to let Kayla go.

Two large, glossy ravens catch my attention as soon as the cab driver deposits me and my suitcases at the Ganges docks. They take wing from the red roof of the coast guard building and land on the sidewalk three feet away from me. We stare at each other, not moving, my blue eyes to their black-pebble orbs. My heart opens wide and releases a tingling flush of gratitude and reverence. I incline my head and touch two fingers to my brow. The ravens respond with a series of guttural croaks and then fly off into the glum, overcast sky.

"Communing with ravens now are you?" says a male voice from behind me, "What are they going to think of you back in Toronto?"

It's Will, with a single, crimson rosebud in one hand and what smells like a bag of Barb's cinnamon twists in the other.

"That's exactly what I've been worrying about," I say, laughing, "What a lovely surprise! But what are you doing here? I thought you were leaving yesterday?"

"I didn't have the heart to go back to Vancouver just yet," he says, "and I wanted to send you home with a bit of sweetness to remember me by. I called the hotel this morning, but you weren't in. I was hoping to catch you before your floatplane left."

"I was up late doing ritual with Kayla and I stayed at her place," I say.

Our hands touch as he passes his gifts to me and a rush of pleasure courses through my nerve endings. He is looking at me in that cocked-head, intense way of his, making me acutely aware of the few inches that separate us at the moment, and the immense distance that will soon separate us.

"There is no way I could ever forget you, Will," I say, lightly brushing my fingertips over his cheek.

The tide is high and the ramp to the floatplane dock is less steep and precarious than when I arrived on Salt Spring. Even so, I've learned my lesson. I'm wearing my flattest-heeled boots and a loose pair of pants. Will carries my luggage while I cling to a bag filled with my Salt Spring treasures: the carved raven, the blue-bead necklace from Emilie, my purple bag and art supplies, a black Goddess statue that Kayla gave me as a parting gift, and Will's rosebud and cinnamon twists.

We stand at the edge of the dock, apart from the other waiting passengers. I fill my lungs with big breaths of the clean, salty air. The ocean is flat calm and a perfect, silver mirror for the cloud-textured sky. The shiny, slick head of a seal follows in the wake of a fishing vessel. Will takes my hand and an electric current hums between us.

"I wish we had more time together," he says, "I'd love to hear about your ritual with Kayla. You look different today, more at peace and even more beautiful."

I tilt my head and stare at him to see if he is joking. From my strict standards, my current state is at the extreme, negative end of the beauty scale: dark, puffy circles under my eyes, chipped nail polish, no make-up, my hair pulled back in a ponytail and sloppy, comfortable clothes. But his admiration seems genuine, and I suspect that Will's appreciation cuts past the surface layers to the deeper, feminine beauty waking up in me.

My stomach lurches as the floatplane comes in for a landing. I grab Will's coat lapels and impulsively kiss him. Not the hot, erotic kiss of the other night, but a hungry, desperate kiss, with my lips pressed hard against his.

"I don't want to go back," I whisper, "I don't want to lose everything that has happened to me here and everyone I've met. I want more of this, more of you."

"Name the place and I'll be there," Will says, pressing his

body close against mine.

"New Year's Eve in Toronto," I say, "Come any time after Christmas and stay with me."

"Yes," Will says, "I'll book it today and let you know."

The pilot holds tight on my elbow as I climb the swaying steps and turn for a final goodbye wave to Will. I perch on the edge of the black leather seat and press my face up against the chilly glass. Will is alone on the dock, his sea green eyes glued to mine. My heart pounds loudly and floods me with a wild longing I've never felt before; I want to know this man, be with him, from my deep insides to his.

Then Will is gone and Salt Spring rapidly vanishes from sight as the plane makes its rattling, shaking escape into the gently weeping sky.

With a grinding thud, the airplane wheels connect with the frozen, unforgiving ground, jolting my hard bones in their soft flesh. The engines roar fiercely, exerting a tremendous, back-thrust power, like a giant beast digging in its heels to slow its forward motion. My lips are dry and cracked and my temples throb to a pained, sluggish tempo. The rumpled businessman crammed next to me wakes up with a snort and a wide yawn, adding a blast of stale beer breath to the recycled air currents.

I flex and wiggle my cramped, ink-stained fingers and gather up my art supplies. I've been sketching non-stop for hours, trying to get what is inside of me onto the empty page — images of a mist-borne raven, Kayla in her red cloak, Hecate stirring Her storytelling cauldron, my Goddess self with the shining ember in her core, and my cupped hands holding four seeds: one jet black, one lily white, one blood red and one shiny gold — but it is not enough to capture my wonder at everything I've experienced, nor to curb the strange sense that I'm not returning home, but more leaving my real home behind.

On one page I've carefully scribed in bold, red ink Kayla's final words when she said goodbye: "We are the ones who are going to change this world — you, me and countless others who are waking to their deeper, spiritual nature. I believe in your beauty and mine, and of every living person. I believe our wounding holds the secrets that can set us free. And I believe the earth is alive and magic is real, and their powers can help us return to our better instincts. This is the new dawn and our shining potential that Ereshkigal and Hecate spoke of. We are the new world we are waiting for. Together we will change our lives and our shared reality, one person, one soul, one healing moment at a time. No one or nothing else can save us."

Everywhere around me, video screens go blank and people look up with equally blank expressions. Is anyone else on this plane waking up in the ways that Kayla speaks of? Are there other fellow travelers of Hecate's path? None of the nearby passengers look beyond the bubble of their seat to make contact with their neighbors. I see tired, burdened people, not kindred spirits wanting to save their souls and heal the world.

The onslaught of passengers catches me up in its momentum as we stream from the plane's compressed interior toward the cavernous baggage area. Everyone is on fast forward, seeming to rush for the sake of rushing. And then we wait, separate little islands of disconnected humanity, for the clunking sounds that announce the arrival of our luggage. People droop over baggage carts loaded down with brightly wrapped presents, and haggard-looking parents struggle to corral their whining kids. No one appears particularly festive, despite the liberal draping of sparkling garlands and giant-proportioned Christmas bobbles that brighten the airport's interior.

I walk around to re-activate my circulation and to fend off my building anxiety. There are too many colliding noises, too many glaring lights and too many foreign smells. I feel myself shutting down and speeding up at the same time as my guts tense and my headache worsens. How am I going to cope with whatever is waiting for me here? My Opa Kass, my beloved Opa, how much longer do I have with him? Is this Christmas our last together? Tears blur my eyes and I rub them away with the back of my hand. And work, my new job, Matt — my heart squeezes and then hardens — maybe I've got Matt wrong, maybe he isn't my friend and ally after all.

My suitcases tumble down onto the luggage carousel and I press through the crowd to retrieve them. I bundle up in my winter coat and walk outside. The frigid night air hits me like a cold slap in the face, and my nostrils contract in a reflexive attempt to shut out the reek of car exhaust and the day's accumulation of smog. I drag my gear to a cab and plunk down in the back seat as the driver tosses my bags into the trunk. I won't part with my bag of Salt Spring treasures and feel the reassuring press of my raven's wooden wings within the protective circle of my left arm. There are no tattooed stars on this driver's neck, nor much warmth and welcome in his obligatory Merry Christmas greeting.

We push our way to the center of the multi-lane highway and join the hive mind that orders the profusion of vehicles speeding forward in the constant glare of headlights and streetlamps. I look out my window for a glimpse of the stars and the wind's movement in the dark silhouettes of trees, but I can only see the towering, box-like shapes of urban, industrial sprawl.

My phone rings when the cab meter hits the twenty-dollar

mark. After days of silence, it's Matt.

"Hi, Sarah. Where are you? Are you back in Toronto?" Matt says in his easy, assured manner, "Sorry to call so late. I tried your phone earlier but I couldn't get through."

"I landed about thirty minutes ago. I'm in a cab heading home," I say, trying to make my voice sound as even as possible, while my backbone stiffens like a ramming pole. I bite back my anger and accusations; I can't let on how much I already know. Damn, why didn't I think this through? What am I supposed to say to him?

"Well welcome back and Merry Christmas," he says, "Can you talk for a bit? There have been things going on in the office. I sent you an e-mail to keep you advised, but I didn't want to bother you with the details on your vacation. I knew you'd be back tonight, so I thought I would try to connect."

I hear quiet strains of jazz in the background and the clinking of ice in a glass. I imagine Matt stretched out in front of the bird's-eye view from his waterfront penthouse, scotch in hand, cool and in control like usual.

"It'd be nice for you to fill me in," I say, keeping my breath slow and even, "I'll admit the e-mail was a tad disturbing."

"Always the master of understatement," Matt says, laughing, "You should be fuming. I would be if I were in your shoes."

Matt's face appears in my mind's eye, with those startling green eyes lit up with mischief and crinkling at the corners. How dare he laugh after the agony he has put me through! I forget my breath. And I don't care that I'm in a cab with the driver listening in on my conversation.

"Then why didn't you contact me sooner?" I say, "And why the hell did you push me to take a vacation?"

"Ah, there's the temper I'm looking for," Matt says, "You should be totally pissed off at me. I'm a coward, calling you rather than meeting you face-to-face. This way you can't throw anything at me. But I promise you, I have a master plan."

A master goddamn plan! Is that what Matt calls those infuriating exchanges with Marsha and Trent?

"Better spill it quick then," I say, "I'm not that far from your place, and I may have to come by and give you a good bash with a hard brick."

"I'm sorry, Sarah. Please let me explain," Matt says, "The vacation idea was to get you out of the office so I could give Marsha enough rope to hang herself. I knew she would be furious about your promotion, especially since I didn't talk to her about it beforehand. And I had a feeling that if I gave her the opportunity, a little nudge, she would try to pull some stunt to undermine you if you weren't around to object."

Matt isn't laughing anymore and he has turned the music off.

"And what was your little nudge?" I say.

"I asked her how the reorganization was going and suggested she might want to give me an update before the holidays," Matt says, "Trent was in the room at the time, and I could see the wheels turning between the two of them."

"So what did she do?" I ask, though I already know the answer thanks to Jules's clandestine activities.

"Exactly what I thought she'd do," Matt says, "She drew up an organization chart and a list of staff changes that totally favor Lead Digital and Trent, and screw things up for you. She even had the audacity to suggest that Brendon work for Trent when he is the obvious candidate for your job."

"And what about Marsha's push to finalize these changes for January before I can have any input?" I ask.

"Now that was the icing on the cake for me," Matt says, "I've known for awhile that she's more than a bit off balance, especially in relation to you. I'm not sure how hard Trent pushed her, but she exceeded my expectations in terms of aggressive stupidity."

Matt rarely keeps secrets from me, at least not professional ones, and I thought I was in the know about his views on everyone in the office. But he has never once let on that he didn't like or trust Marsha. I rotate my neck gently from left to right, releasing a bit of the built-up tension, and relax my grip on the phone.

"So you don't agree with any of this?" I say.

"Are you kidding?" Matt says, "It's pure madness to mix up the TechStar and Lead Digital teams; they'd be at each others' throats in a week's time. From our conversations, I understand that's your opinion as well."

"Absolutely," I say, "And Marsha knows this. I've been clear that we need to keep the staff groups separate."

"Have you documented these discussions with Marsha?" Matt says.

"Of course," I say.

"Yes, that's my Sarah!" Matt says, "Send me what you've got."

"And what happens next?" I ask.

"Leave that to me," Matt says, "I've kept Marsha hanging until after Christmas to see if she will build up a little more steam. And then I'll figure out best tactics. I'll let you know before you come back in January."

The cab is now zooming along the Gardiner Expressway between solid masses of water-view condominiums on either side of the highway. Matt is somewhere amongst those high-up, twinkling lights, perhaps even looking down on me this very instant. I hear the muted sounds of his movements through the phone and the even rise and fall of his breath. The brittle, hard place inside of me, the one that had crusted around my sweet spot for Matt, begins to soften.

"How long have you been planning this?" I say.

"From the second I figured out who was behind the nasty rumors about you," Matt says.

"You mean the ones about me sleeping with you and with Steve?" I say.

"Those would be the ones," Matt says, "Look, I'm the one who got us into this painful merger. It has already cost us Steve and I don't want to lose you. If anyone is going down, it's Marsha."

"God, Matt, your e-mail really messed with my head," I say with a short, sharp laugh, "I thought you had joined the enemies' camp! And now I don't know whether to punch you or kiss you."

"I'd never be your enemy, Sarah, never; I'm just the opposite," Matt says, and there is something unexpected in his voice, a lover's caress, and it sets my pulse racing, "If I have a choice in the matter, I'll take the kiss."

Dead silence. A different kind of tension, delicious and sizzling, fires up my lower regions.

And then Matt starts to laugh, "I can't believe I said that! Now you're really going to hit me with a brick. I am doubly sorry, Sarah! Please wipe that last remark from your memory bank."

Perhaps I can erase my mental memory, but the heat between my legs won't be forgetting this exchange soon.

Our call ends as the driver turns off the highway into the downtown core. Kayla is right, things are never as they appear on the surface. Matt is not my enemy, but a secret admirer. Marsha is not my nemesis, but a spider caught in her own web. And maybe I need to listen to Opa Kass and enjoy the time we have left together, rather than wasting it crying over something that can't be changed. How many other things have I misconstrued?

I wipe the steam away from the cab window and peer out at the familiar landscape. Splashes of colored lights adorn streetlamps, cranes, storefronts and office buildings, adding beauty and magic to these everyday surfaces. Tonight I will sleep in my own bed with its lavender-scented sheets and pretty, floral duvet. Tomorrow I will celebrate Christmas with my Opa and show him my new sketchbook. Next week I'll share a bottle of wine with Jules and spill out the details of my great adventure. Will, sweet, sexy, intriguing Will, is spending New Year's Eve with me. And who knows what beginnings and changes January will bring?

With closed eyes, I let the hum of the taxi wheels on the pavement lull me into a deeper state of relaxation. After a few slow, measured breaths, I slip into my inner landscape and a dream vision opens before me.

A raven caws from a shadowy tree in the far distance of this twilight realm. I am standing at a crossroads; two roadways intersect at my feet: one is from downtown Toronto, with the skyscrapers and storefronts where I work, and the other is the winding, forest-edged road that leads to Kayla's house. I feel a gentle nudge in the small of my back, and though I can't see anyone, I hear the dog-man's voice inside my head, "Time to choose, Sarah-woman."

"I choose the middle way, the Dark Goddess's Path of She," I say without a pause.

The two roads blend and merge, and then there is only one path, hewn of red granite paving stones, flecked with tiny glimmers of silver light. I sniff the air to take in its guiding currents. Wafts of smoky, pungent fumes curl under my nostrils and beckon me toward Her waiting cauldron brew and its storytelling magic.

"I am coming, Hecate," I cry out, "I am coming!"

And then, with a quickening heart, I take my first step forward into the rest of my life.

ACKNOWLEDGEMENTS

Tale of the Lost Daughter was born of my profound journey with the Dark Goddess Hecate. She first came to me in a dream in my mid-twenties and I have been traveling with Her ever since. It is Her mysteries and ways that infuse my Path of She writings and Sarah's journey in *Tale of the Lost Daughter*.

This book would not have been possible without the extraordinary, unending support and love of my partner Larry and my son Nathan. I would also like to thank Shelby Johnstone for her creative genius in designing the book cover, Kathy Page for her brilliant editorial feedback and Christina Antonick whose magical hands grace the cover. My sincere thanks go out to: my core band of cheerleaders and first readers who have believed in this project and in me: Jean Clark, Brian Clark, Julie Clark, Jennifer Lind, Jordan Jackson, Laura Scott, Suzanne Michelle, Elizabeth Flannigan, Lisa Lipsett, Rebecca Niedziela, Brenda Guild and Audrey Moon; and to my Salt Spring pagan companions for the powerful, delicious magic we have woven together over many years.

I am also indebted to my key spiritual influences: Vipassana Insight Meditation and the Buddhist writings and teachings of Dhiravamsa and Andy James; and the Reclaiming Tradition of Witchcraft, the teachings of the Reclaiming community and the writings of Starhawk.

About the Author

Karen Clark is the author of *Tale of the Lost Daughter*, *The Path of She Book of Sabbats: A Journey of Soul Across the Seasons*, and the *Path of She Guided Journey Series*. As a writer, teacher and waking woman, Karen's passion is to return the Goddess and our sacred feminine nature back to their rightful place in our everyday lives.

Karen's Path of She work translates Goddess mysteries to our modern search for meaning, healing, personal growth, and collective transformation.

About the Path of She

The Path of She invites you on a journey of transformation with the Goddess to reclaim Her life-giving ways, and your true, beautiful Self. Rooted in Goddess wisdom teachings, the Path of She can inspire and guide your travels on this ancient pathway, providing you with the knowledge, skills and experiences to heal and transform your life and our world.

To learn more about Karen and the Path of She, visit: **pathofshe.com** where you can subscribe to receive posts by email or listen to Path of She podcasts.

Follow Path of She on: **Facebook, Twitter, Itunes and Android.**

BOOKS IN THE PATH OF SHE SERIES

GUIDED JOURNEY SERIES

Each season expresses different aspects of the elemental forces that shape life on Earth, written large in the physical displays of Nature, and the Goddess mysteries that illuminate our human experience and life story.

Align your journey of soul with these seasonal offerings of Nature and the Goddess through a seven-lesson guided journey with integrated wisdom teachings, pathwork exercises, journaling tasks and a guided meditation.

Fall Journey

Your Hera's Path: Seeking Your Spiritual Roots

Winter Journey

Your Rebirth Magic: Braving the Great Below

Spring Journey

Your Whole/Holy Powers: Embracing Your Life Story

Summer Journey

Thou Art Goddess: Claiming Your Inner Goddess

AVAILABLE AT THE PATH STORE

https://pathofshe.com/path-store/

OTHER PATH OF SHE BOOKS

The Path of She Book of Sabbats: A Journey of Soul Across the Seasons

With Nature and the Gods and Goddesses as your guides, travel through the eight pagan Sabbats that mark the four seasons and their midway points.

Connect your spiritual path with the energy of the Earth through teachings, guided meditations and pathwork exercises. Explore your soul's journey through its seasons of light, dark, life, death, joy and sorrow. Embrace the powerful, essential work of transforming your life. Find your way home to your true, beautiful Self.

Find out more about Path of She books and other offerings at the Path Store: pathofshe.com/path-store/

Made in the USA
Monee, IL
07 July 2020